FATHERING

FATHERING

Strengthening Connection
With Your Children
No Matter Where You Are

Will Glennon

CONARI PRESS
Berkeley, CA

Conari Press books are distributed by Publishers Group West

ISBN: 1-57324-002-8

Cover design: Karen Bouris and Generic Type
Cover photo: Bill Carter

Library of Congress Cataloging-in-Publication Data
Glennon, Will, 1949–
Fathering : strengthening connection with your children
no matter where you are / Will Glennon.
p.   cm.
ISBN 1-57324-002-8 (trade paper) : $12.95
1. Fatherhood—Psychological aspects.
2. Father and child.   3. Parenting.
HQ756.G55   1995
306.874'2—dc20   95-3726

Printed in the United States of America on recycled paper

4 6 8 10 9 7 5

Acknowledgments

*I am deeply grateful to all the fathers who
so generously shared their time and experiences
and who so thoroughly and fearlessly
bared even the most painful parts of their lives to me.*

To my father William Glennon
for teaching me the power
and potential of father

❖

To Mary Jane Ryan
for honoring a father's
choice to parent

❖

And to Damian and Rachelle
for making it all
so wonderfully rewarding.

Contents

Foreword

Dad, Father, Pops. Allow yourself a moment to think of the man you've called Father. Capture an image of him from your childhood—in his favorite chair, the way he dressed, his characteristic look or mood, perhaps the smell of his cologne or tobacco. Do you recall the power he had to delight you with his approval, to create dread in you with his displeasure, or to wound you with his indifference? Did you ever stay awake just to hear his voice when he came home, or did you ever long for his attention or praise?

Do you have children? Can you imagine that even at a young age, they will already have longings, images, and dreads regarding you? One day these will become old memories of delightful things you said and did, your characteristic moods, perhaps even the hurtful things you did or didn't do. *Father* will become a powerful, evocative word for your children like your father is for you.

Will Glennon's book, *Fathering*, is based on sound psychological principles, but it speaks to the heart. Though it is a book about fathers and fathering, it is not a traditional "how-to" manual. Using short but powerful vignettes, from fathers from all walks of life, he stirs memories of childhoods, fathers, and being or not being fathered. Allowing us to have empathy for ourselves as children, he subtly challenges us to feel the impact we have on our children.

Many men are capable of numbing their emotions, of becoming stoic problem solvers and unemotional security providers. However, it is feeling what our children feel, having the discipline to walk beside them rather than always lead, and having the courage to set a good example that are the hallmarks of what fathering needs to be today.

Many of today's fathers were often poorly trained by their own fathers to be modern coaches, that is, loving, enjoying, cajoling, and disciplining (as opposed to punishing) their children to become capable, productive people who enjoy loving and being loved. By allowing men to tell their father stories, the author avoids the masculine tendency to teach "the facts." Rather, the stories speak for themselves, teaching through feeling that the best way to father is to enjoy our children and coach them into being enjoyable when they are not. How could a child feel insecure if she felt that she was a source of pleasure to her parents?

Isn't the most secure form of bond that of being enjoyed? It does take work to raise a child that both others and parents can truly delight in. What a long way we will have come if most of us can do that!

Richard W. Levak, Ph.D.
Psychologist

Chapter 1

The Crisis in Fathering

My father was a very serious man. I used to make up all kinds of explanations, excuses really, for why he was the way he was. The truth is I don't care about the reasons anymore. He died without ever telling me he loved me, without ever hugging me, without ever saying he was proud of me. I still don't understand it. It's like there is this giant hole inside of me that can never be filled.

Fathering. It's not a word we're comfortable with. It feels awkward and sounds funny. It isn't even in most dictionaries. While the concept exists as a logical counterpoint to mothering, we as a society seem at a loss for any sense of what it really represents. That fact is at the heart of a profoundly devastating wound for many men: We have lost our fathers, and far too many of us who are fathers are in serious danger of losing our children.

To cite just one of myriad statistics indicating the problem, a recent study found that only 20 percent of the fathers surveyed felt that they had a close emotional relationship with *either* their fathers or their sons.[1] That is a remarkable piece of information. In this statistically saturated world, it is easy to let the flood of numbers simply roll on. But we as men, as fathers, must force ourselves to stop for a moment and look beyond the numbers to see the very real human suffering—ours and that of those we love—that this particular statistic suggests: The vast majority of men in this country are emotionally distant, disconnected from their closest male relatives.

In general, men tend to be very good at controlling their feelings. We are particularly good at "getting on with things" in the face of hardship, danger, pain, and turmoil. It is our training, our history, and even our mythology, weaned as we were on larger-than-life heroes stoically pushing forward to overcome enormous difficulties and crippling losses.

This skill, this ability to function effectively in the face of emotional pressure, has served us well, but it has also exacted a very dear price. It has allowed us to create and accomplish out in the world with single-minded focus; but, largely unnoticed, it has also forced many of us to lose track of what is most important and precious, the reasons why we work so hard and what we are working for—our loved ones.

In homes all across the country, men are "getting on" with the business of living. But, as the statistics painfully demonstrate, in four out of five of those homes, they are doing it without the reassuringly deep comfort of a close emotional relationship with either their father or their children.

My Dad worked himself to death. He dropped out of school when he was fourteen to get a job to put food on his mother's table, and he just never stopped. It was like he was afraid that if he ever slowed down, everything would fall apart. He had never known how to be a kid and he sure didn't know how to be with a kid; it was like living with an alien. I didn't know him well but I loved him. It still makes me sad to think about him. Sometimes I would catch him looking at me or my brother with this incredibly sad look on his face, like he knew something was missing, but it was beyond his ability to deal with it.

This book is about something that is difficult to describe—the close and powerful emotional connection that flows like a current of electricity between a father and his children. It is a most powerful thing and a most fragile one. It can be lost or interrupted abruptly, or it can persist over vast distances and time. It can make the difference between a life that is rich and full and one that is empty and meaningless. It is one of our deepest desires as men yet, for so many of us, it has proven to be painfully elusive.

For too long we have been silent about our love for our

children, about the happiness and sorrow that being a father brings. *Fathering: Strengthening Connection with Your Children No Matter Where You Are* seeks to break the silence by weaving together men's stories about the joy and pain of being a father. These stories, told by fathers whose collective wisdom and experience is represented on these pages, appear as italicized sections. They are anonymous because the cloak of anonymity gave men the freedom to fully explore these deeply emotional issues. These stories—heart-wrenching, impassioned, and honest—represent the collective voice of today's father. The narrative that flows from their stories is my attempt to record what I have learned from these men, from their efforts and their anguish.

> *I don't remember very much about my childhood— there are so many reasons to forget. My father was never home. Sometimes when I was already in bed and supposed to be asleep, I'd stay awake just to hear his voice when he came in. Even on weekends, I hardly ever saw him, except for when we would all dress up and go to church on Sunday. My parents broke up when I was twelve, and he just sort of faded away. My mother still tells me he is a good man, but how would I know?*

The emotional distance that has increasingly come to characterize men's lives has begun to reverberate out into the world. A second set of statistics[2] tells us that nearly 49.8 percent of our children live outside traditional two-parent homes; that fathers in the United States spend less time with their children than in any other country; and that among those fathers who do live with their children, the average amount of time spent with them is twelve minutes per day.

These are frightening signposts proclaiming a crisis of monumental proportions. We have allowed ourselves and our children to drift, like untethered astronauts, farther and farther away from the heartbeat of our humanity. We have sentenced our children to the bewildering experience of growing up with a desperate need to feel loved by a father who all too often is simply not there, either physically or emotionally.

There are even more statistics—ones that reveal the devastating ripple effects on society of absent fathers who fail to forge strong emotional ties to their children. These statistics are the most frightening of all, because they are, by definition, so impersonal and, tragically, so irrevocable: Nearly 80 percent of those who end up in our juvenile justice system lived in homes without a father; the overwhelming majority of our adult prison population grew up without fathers; the single strongest predictor of violent juvenile crime, specifically robbery and murder, is that the child grew up without a close relationship to his father.[3]

The statistics don't lie. We *are* in a crisis of major proportions, and the casualties—both parents and children—are increasing at an alarming rate. We find ourselves at a juncture in time, where a staggering proportion of men feel distant and alone, each of us, like the boy in the hermetically sealed bubble, moving through life separated from everyone else by some inexplicable, invisible barrier. It begins when we are just boys, too often boys without the fathers we need, and it persists when we grow up, becoming fathers ourselves and, out of ignorance, re-creating the cycle of distance with our own children. And we've reached this place despite the fact that none of us ever wanted to be here.

> *My children are all grown and have families of their own. I rarely see them and when I do, it is usually strained and awkward. I know that it is mostly my fault because I was never there when they were young, but that doesn't make it any easier.*
>
> *I just wish I knew back when I was a young father what I know now. When I finally realized what was really important to me—my kids—I had to face the reality that I had done this to myself.*

It is the absence of the father—physically and, much more important, emotionally—that is at the heart of the crisis. Paradoxically, however, it is the miracle of becoming a father that opens up for us the most inviting, most surprising, and most promising avenue for finding our way back to our hearts and souls. Fatherhood is a precious opportunity, and we know it, even if we cannot comprehend or articulate why. It is something we feel in our bones. We want to understand it, to face the challenge and be found worthy; we know that there is something to it that can transform us if only we do it right, but often we don't even know how to begin.

Out of fear, out of ignorance, it is easiest to gravitate toward the patterns of fathering in which we were raised. From the birth of our first child, we tend to concede the role of comforter and nurturer to our wives and find ourselves removed from our child. The family dynamic becomes established, and we find ourselves somehow inexplicably "outside." For most of us it is not a good place to be, but we feel powerless to change it; we don't even have a vocabulary for how to talk about it. It is just a feeling, a very deep and painful feeling, but talking about our feelings is not something with which men are terribly comfortable.

This distance, which has been created slowly and silently, can no longer be tolerated. Somehow now, not tomorrow, not next year, we need to begin to forge a path back to ourselves and our children, to discover how to create and maintain deep and strong emotional connections with them.

In retrospect, it is astounding that we could have allowed things to deteriorate so dramatically without noticing. As painful as it might be to admit, sometimes life must deliver us a solid blow to the solar plexus before we get the point. For many men that blow comes with divorce, when distance becomes an inescapable result, and they are suddenly faced with the bleak probability that the strength of their connection to their children will be severely tested.

The pain I was feeling and that of my ex-wife, I reckoned, were our just desserts for the situation we had conspired to land ourselves in. But the boys, then just three and five, could scarcely be expected to understand what was going on. I wept loudly each evening as I drove to a strange apartment with the grief and bewilderment of these two innocents foremost in my mind. I had no idea what to do—no road map, little guidance, and precious few positive stories to tell myself about what was happening. Instead I could count on only an act of faith, a fool's promise perhaps. I could hear the song going round in my head, "Everything's gonna be all right, everything's gonna be all right."

For many men, divorce is a defining moment. Standing amid the rubble of shattered illusions, broken promises, and best intentions gone awry, it can be a time of painful clarity if faced courageously and honestly. Over and over in these pages, the one issue that surfaces with overwhelming power for men is the absolute terror at the prospect of losing their children through divorce. It is from this battered emotional outpost that the crisis looms clear and threatening, and it is largely from these men, struggling to come to grips with how to maintain and nurture a connection to their children, and from the growing ranks of full-time fathers, often treated as an oddity rather than the pioneers they are, that the alarm is being sounded.

This book is a report from men on the front line. The original inspiration came from Denys Candy, a friend and father who has grappled with maintaining strong bonds with his children despite the distance imposed by divorce.

Since this has been my experience also—I was divorced when my children were very young and, for the past sixteen years, I too have searched for ways to remain connected—Denys's idea struck a cord. I began to search out other fathers—eventually interviewing more than a hundred—young, old, and in between, and in all kinds of circumstances: still married and living with their children, divorced, single, remarried with stepchildren, even some grandfathers. I wanted to find out what they had learned about how to be a good father. More important and somewhat surprising, I also learned how they felt about their own fathers and the process of fathering itself.

What I found initially was alarming. Although one of the most important goals of almost every father I spoke with was to have a close relationship with his children, when it came to knowing how to get there, far too many men admitted being at a painful loss. But I also found something quite hopeful that makes up the heart of this book: a depth of feeling and openness that was powerful and consistent. The answers may not always be clear, but the commitment to finding them was unwavering.

I've also come to see that when discussing fathering there are no experts. There are only men who have tried to do their best and are willing to share their experience—their accomplishments and their failures, their heartaches and their joys, their confusion and their clarity.

There are no secret answers. Building and nurturing a father-child relationship requires the knowledge that it can be done, the commitment that it will be done, the persistence to keep on trying, and the courage to do whatever is necessary to make sure it does get done.

The next two chapters explore how we got here, first from a social and then a more personal level, with the belief that this understanding is important only in that it can help us ease our way back out. This is not a time or a place to assess fault—and it would a heartless and futile undertaking. What we need is not the paralysis of guilt or the distraction of assigning blame, but rather the commitment to not let ourselves and our children continue to drift apart, encouragement and support from those who are finding their way back, and bold signposts to help us on our way.

With this book, the one hundred of us hope to at least make a start: to explore the problems that fathers face, and to identify the things we need to do, the feelings we need to become more comfortable with, the parts of our role as fathers that we need to have a deeper understanding of, and the mistakes we need to avoid in order to nurture our relationship with our children.

We can make *fathering* a word that is as comfortable as *mothering,* one that evokes warmth, strength, security, and a deep unbreakable bond of love. But it will take understanding and courage.

NOTES

1. Osherson, S., *Finding Our Fathers: The Unfinished Business of Manhood.*
2. U.S. Census Report; Princeton Survey Research.
3. U.S. Department of Justice; California Youth Authority; National Council on Crime and Delinquency

Chapter 2

Caught in the Currents
of Change

I was working out of town for nearly two full months last year, living at a hotel where a lot of other men working on the same project were staying. It was kind of an unusual situation because we were all strangers, from very different backgrounds, but we would work together all day and then see each other at the hotel restaurant and bar each night. For the most part, they were men that normally I would probably never say more than a few words to, but because of the circumstances I ended up getting to know quite a few of them pretty well.

When the conversations finally got around to their children—which was only long after we had exhausted all the sports conversations we could come up with, and usually after a fair number of drinks—I can't tell you how many of these guy were just baffled, almost shell-shocked. They loved their kids, they would swell up with pride just talking about them, but at the same time there was this huge empty space. They'd joke about not being able to understand babies or teenagers, or about not knowing how to play with little kids. They'd tell me how "good" the wife was with their daughter, or their son, or their kids. They'd complain about not having more time to take the kid out to the ballpark. But underneath it all was this very sad sense of loss. It's like they knew something was missing but couldn't put their finger on just what it was or how to find it.

Something unusual has been going on recently—people are starting to talk about fathers. Unfortunately, as is so often the case when the bright lights of attention are suddenly turned on, much of the commentary is decisively negative. As noted in chapter 1, a flood of studies have been released, documenting in stark detail the absence of fathers, physically and emotionally, and bringing into sharp focus the increasingly long list of ugly consequences.

Mothers, who have traditionally taken the rap for screwing up the kids because, after all, they were there, are suddenly being afforded a little relief. The focus of blame is shifting to fathers because so often they are not there. Even the politicians are jumping into the debate, decrying "deadbeat dads" as the root of virtually all social ills, and calling for a "return" to family values.

Unfortunately, our first instinct when confronted with a problem—particularly one of the magnitude and with the implications as this—is to rush to assign blame. But if we look with our hearts instead of our fear, if we seek a path out of the suffering instead of simply a scapegoat, what we must face is that the absent father—both the one who is not physically there as well as the one who is not present emotionally—is a tragic consequence of the times we live in.

Like it or not, we are in the midst of a major economic, social, and cultural transition. The roles of men and women and therefore the roles of mothers and fathers are changing—and changing rapidly. These changes stem in part from new and often courageous choices being made by the emerging generations of women and men, and also in part from the very impersonal and inexorable economic shifts taking place. What we want, need, and expect from our most intimate relationships is being reexamined and redefined as we go. At the same time, women are moving into the workplace at an astonishing rate, out of both choice and necessity. The result is a boiling cauldron of change in the most vulnerable places in our lives; and one of the most visible casualties is the tragedy of the absent father, whether in another city, another home, another room, or simply always at work.

Change is difficult and painful. Painful because the ways of the past now appear sadly inadequate. Painful because what should replace the ways of the past is not at all clear.

And painful because, regardless of the wounds, the constraints, injustices, or inadequacies of the "old way," there were also benefits, particularly the comfort of familiarity. Painful or not, these changes are upon us. Whether we applaud, fear, or resent them no longer matters; they are here and we must deal with them.

Nowhere are the sweeping changes that have, in a few short generations, transformed the map of family structures more evident than in divorce rates. Today, half of all marriages end in divorce, and, for the most part, the children of divorce stay with their mothers. The fathers end up separated from their children, without any model or support system teaching them how to stay connected and, even more tragic, often without the emotional preparation or resources to fashion a new pathway back.

Although the sharp severance of divorce is frequently the wake-up call that prompts fathers to redouble their efforts to maintain a strong connection to their children, unfortunately, just as often it is the final push that sends an already precariously connected father out into a distant and lonely orbit.

It was so hard. When my wife and I broke up, it was like the earth opened up and destroyed everything. My children were very young and my ex-wife was very bitter. She wanted revenge, she wanted money, and she wanted to hurt me. The only way she knew how to get at me was to keep me from my kids. She wouldn't let me see them; when I stopped by day care to see the kids, she called the police and said I was trying to kidnap them. It got so horrible that I finally decided to leave town in the hope that things would quiet down.

When I called a few months later to try to work out some kind of visitation schedule, she accused me of abandoning them. I know I'm far from perfect and I screwed up enough myself, but she made it so hard I finally gave up.

Divorce statistics do not begin to reveal the challenge we as fathers face. For even if we are not physically separated from our children, what is expected of us as fathers—from our wives, from our children, and even from ourselves—is very different from the model we grew up with. Traditionally in this culture, our role—stoic, brave, silent—has been defined by emotional distance. Not that we didn't each have a deep well of feelings, but far too often those feelings were locked away in an inaccessible place. Too many fathers are skilled in work, in providing, in disciplining, but are untrained, unsupported, unsure, and uneasy in the crucial task of nurturing. The distance our fathers accepted as natural and appropriate is now threatening to unravel the very social fabric of parenting. The simplistic response to this by many men is an angry rejection of the "old ways," most often expressed in some variation of "I won't make the mistakes my father made."

My father is not the warmest and most expressive guy in the world, but he has kept his mind open and has accumulated a lot of wisdom in his years. One day, shortly after my son was born, my father and I were talking. I got somewhat carried away with my resolve that I would not be as emotionally withdrawn as he had been. He listened politely and then said, "Son, I've made my mistakes as a father; now it's your turn."

It is true that if we are smart enough, courageous enough, persistent enough, and vigilant enough, we won't make the same mistakes our fathers made—we will make our own mistakes. But before we toss out our fathers with last year's calendar, it might help to remember that they grew up in another time, and in a very real sense pioneered a new era.

This is more true today than it has ever been. Television, jet airplanes, telephones, copiers and fax machines, personal computers, the list goes on and on—all are essential fixtures in our lifetime that did not exist when most of our fathers were growing up. And, of course, their most important lessons about fathering came from their fathers, many of whom were born in the nineteenth century. We can turn our backs in hurt and anger at the fathering style we were handed, but that would be wrong, it would be wasteful, and it would be disrespectful.

I tried so many times to get through to the old man. I tried logic, humor, veiled threats; I even tried taking away the thing he wanted the most—contact with his grandchildren. He's just scared. The rules have changed, and he thinks that for him to even admit that there may be another way to do things than the way he did is to admit he was wrong. I don't expect him to change who he is; I just want him to accept me for who I am.

Despite what anger or sorrow we may have at how we were fathered, we can't afford to carelessly discard the hard-won lessons of our fathers. We need to take the best of what they gave us as we plot a course toward a new kind of fathering—one built on strong bonds of love, that is expansive and courageous, and that will bring us back into the richness of a deep emotional connection with our children.

If we ask people to select words to positively describe what it means to be a mother, invariably they come up with such terms as nurturing, compassionate, caring, and comforting. For father, the words are protector, provider, responsible, dependable, hardworking, and problem solving. Those characteristics fit well with our culturally projected father images, such as those portrayed in *Leave it to Beaver* and *Father Knows Best.* Ward and Tom are portrayed as kind and understanding men who are primarily problem solvers, that is, men who diffuse and avoid emotional situations by presenting real-world solutions.

If we combine the above terminology of mother and father qualities, it makes up an impressive résumé for good parenting. Traditionally, however, that list has been divided up by gender, with women assigned the internal or emo-

tional tasks and men assigned the external tasks of dealing
with the outside world. This division has deep roots in our
history but, for better and for worse, it is rapidly deteriorat-
ing. The radically changing nature of what it means to be a
man or a woman is not news, but it is a constant source of
challenge and opportunity.

> *My father was a true believer in a clear and rigid
> division of labor—there was women's work and then
> there was men's. He went to work, paid the bills, and
> took care of the yard, while Mom did all the cooking,
> cleaning, and housework. What is weird is that my
> sister being a lawyer and me cooking for a living
> doesn't seem to bother him at all. It's like his rules
> stopped with his generation.*

Over the past thirty years it's become obvious that women
are no longer content to live within the boundaries of
traditional gender roles which severely limit the scope and
magnitude of their dreams. What is now becoming evident
is that men also cannot continue to blindly play out their
appointed roles without increasingly disastrous consequences
to their own emotional health and to that of their children.

> *It's hard. I have everything I'm supposed to have, from
> the good job, nice home, and new car to a loving wife
> and two beautiful kids, and yet I feel trapped in a vise
> that just keeps getting tighter and tighter. My job
> brings in good money, but it takes all my time and*

drains all my energy until there is nothing left. There
has to be more to it. There has to be a better way.

When we examine social evolution in more detail, at least
some of the reason for the urgency in dealing with the
changing role of fathers begins to emerge. For although the
traditional roles of mothers and fathers may appear clear and
defined, in practice they were never as stark nor as isolating
as they appear to us today.

Until relatively recently—the past hundred years or so—
men and women carried out their roles in close and constant
contact with each other and with their children, whether on
a small farm or running a small business or shop. Indeed, for
most of our history, men and women worked side by side—
undertaking different tasks, but performing them in a manner that involved continuous interaction, feedback, and
assistance.

Dad was indeed the protector and provider, but he was
also right there, downstairs in the shop or out in the field,
preparing it for next season's crop. More often than not, Dad
was there every day for the noontime meal, as well as for
breakfast and supper, and the opportunities (and indeed the
obligation) for children to spend time with Dad by helping
out in the fields or in the store were common.

Fathers fulfilled their role in frequent daily contact with
their children, and that contact nurtured the kinds of emotional connections that can only come with the investment
of time. That began to change in our great-grandfathers' and
grandfathers' time, as swelling waves of refugees fled the

poverty of the countryside to find work in the factories and offices of cities around the world.

Increasingly, this new economic reality found fathers leaving home early in the morning and not returning until late at night. The thread of daily contact with their children was lost, as was the constant contact between husband and wife. The division of labor between men and women, which in the past had existed as a relatively intimate partnership, become a division in time and place as well. Fathers were increasingly removed from the home, and mothers became more isolated from the workaday world. This everyday forced distance became the true rupture with the past.

It is impossible to overemphasize the importance of this change. For in building and maintaining close personal relationships, time is a key ingredient, and it is our time with our fathers when we were growing up, as well as with our children as they are growing up, that has been taken away from us.

My father never got over the Great Depression. He had a small business and, almost overnight, he lost it all. He lived every remaining day of his life terrified that he would not be able to provide for his family. The irony was that because he worked so hard to give us what he thought we should have, he was never home. In the end, it killed him.

We don't live our lives in isolation from these larger social conditions. We don't make the rules and we aren't even given a decent map to go by. The vast flow of history, with its wave after wave of social and economic change, has established the conditions under which our lives must be lived. We would like to believe that we have more control over our lives, but time and experience prove to us again and again that the most we can do is choose how we will respond to the circumstances we are presented with.

Fathers today, young and old, have been dealt a very difficult hand. Because of the massive social and economic migrations over the past hundred years, as a group we have been deprived of the daily close contact with our fathers and our children that many of our grandfathers and most of their fathers enjoyed.

Separated from both our fathers and our children, we have been cut off from the heart of the fathering traditions of the past, and have been handed a decidedly garbled message about how we should go about being good fathers today.

Mostly we are unsure of how to proceed. The message that comes through the loudest and resonates the strongest is that we must be protectors and providers. The image of the father as protector and provider is so deeply ingrained in our cultural heritage that it feels as though failing at this means risking one's identity as a man. And so we throw ourselves into the role with fierce determination, as though fulfilling this aspect of our identity as fathers is enough.

When my wife got pregnant with my first daughter, I thought my life was over, and in many ways it was.

Any thoughts I had of being able to finish my educa-
tion or consider music as a career were gone. I was still
very much in love with my wife and wanted to love my
new daughter, but my job was precarious and my skills
were pretty minimal. I was afraid we were about to
enter a life of poverty and insecurity. The only thing
that kept us going was my committing to seventy-hour
workweeks for almost ten years. My wife and I once
calculated that I had seen my oldest daughter awake
less than twelve hours in the first five years of her life.
I will never know if I truly foresaw that miserable fate
or if this was just a self-fulfilling prophesy.

For most men, it is when our children are very young that we
need to work the hardest. We are new on the job, often
insecure about our work identity, and need to put in long
hours to become better at what we do, to become more
valuable to the company, to be recognized as an important
employee. Out of fear, insecurity, and need, we put in long
hours at work and have precious little time left to spend with
our children.

Before we know it, the tiny creatures we brought home
from the hospital are crawling, then walking, then running
to greet us at the door each evening. And as they grow, so too
do their needs—clothes, shoes, medical bills, braces, piano
lessons, judo classes. This is also frequently the time in our
career when we have greater opportunities for advancement,
and that, of course, means even more attention to work,
more hours spent on the job, and more work being brought
home to intrude on the few hours available for our children.

Even men who start out intending to do it differently find themselves in the provider trap.

> *When my son was born, I was determined to do it differently. I took a six-month sabbatical from work to care for him when he was an infant. I did diapers, 2 a.m. feedings, stroller walks in the park—everything. Later, I was the only guy in sight at the day-care center. As he got older, I became increasingly concerned about our finances. We needed a house, I had to start worrying about college tuition . . . I ended up taking a high-powered, well-paying job two hours away from home. When I wasn't driving back and forth, I was flying all over the state, working sixty-hour weeks.*
>
> *Suddenly, it was only my wife at my son's tennis lessons, baseball games, and school recitals. Ten years went by in the blink of an eye: We had financial security, but I missed out on a tremendous amount of my son's life. He never says anything about it, but I know he felt very hurt and abandoned.*

Even when we are home, it is all too often in a state of utter exhaustion. We want, need, and feel we deserve some peace, some time to relax, to unwind and do nothing. To our children, however, that time is experienced very differently. They have gone all day without seeing, talking, or playing with Daddy, and children are not particularly patient. By time you walk in the door, tired, stressed, and in need of quiet, they are ready to jump you in an explosion of enthusiasm.

Sometimes I'd be so wound-up I just knew I couldn't handle the onslaught, so I'd call home and put off my arrival for an hour. Then I'd drive to this really beautiful park a few miles away and just sit there until I could feel the stress drain away. Sometimes it only took a few minutes, and then instead of dreading walking in the door, I couldn't wait.

Because we love our children so much, we want desperately to be good providers and so we work very hard at it. Then suddenly we find ourselves deep into the middle years of our children's youth, at a distance we never planned for nor wanted. We find ourselves on the outside looking in at their lives—their rhythms and schedules—much of which is constructed without concern for our presence, because in truth it is very difficult to assure them we will be there. We try. We try to get to the soccer match, to show up at the parent/teacher night, to get home early so we can play catch, but it is very difficult. They learn to stop counting on us to be there in order not to feel the sharp sting of disappointment, and we end up feeling left out.

Time is important, whether we want it to be or not. The more time we spend working, the more energy we pour into our job, the more all-consuming it can become. Without our ever intending it, work can assume a larger and larger piece of our self-image. It can absorb so much of our identity that it becomes the only thing from which we can derive satisfaction, the only place we feel appreciated. If we are particularly good at our job, it can also become the place where our accomplishments are honored and acknowledged—the center of our feelings of self-worth.

> *I remember back when my children were growing up, I used to go out with the guys from the office for drinks every night. I'd be the first one to volunteer for the out-of-town business trip, the last one to leave the office at night. Now I want to go back, shake myself, and ask what I thought I was doing. The sad thing is I already know. I spent so much time at work and so little time at home that I was simply more comfortable at work. When I went home, it was like entering a foreign country run by a woman I no longer knew and kids I didn't know how to relate to.*

The less time we spend at home, the less familiar it becomes. We lose track of what is going on in our children's lives. We don't know the names of their friends, whom they are feuding with, what they like, or what is bothering them. It can be very disconcerting to listen to your six-year-old explaining an event of crucial importance to him and realize that you know neither the landscape nor the actors.

Like a small crack on the windshield left untended, this lack of involvement can widen and worsen as our children begin to express their anger over our absence in any number of creative ways that are guaranteed to make time spent at

home even less enjoyable. This can become just one more
pressure pushing us farther away, or it can be the wake-up
call that something needs to change.

> *My business had reached a point where it was ready to
> go to another level completely, but to get there would
> have required me to be out of state on a regular basis.
> At the same time, things at home were not doing
> terribly well. My son was starting to get into trouble—
> nothing major, but it was very clear handwriting on
> the wall. I made a decision to restructure my business
> so that I would be able to spend more time at home.
> It meant less money, and at times I have had to really
> stretch to make it work, but I have never regretted my
> decision.*

Unfortunately, we don't all have the ability to unilaterally
restructure our work life and still be able to pay the bills, but
we are all faced with the same dilemma. For the most part,
the very job opportunities available to us that allow us to
provide for our children threaten to pull us so far apart from
them that we might lose the very thing we are working so
hard to maintain—our family. And until recently, there was
very little acknowledgment of this issue by employers.

Balancing work and family life is a very real and difficult
problem with no simple solutions. We cannot return en
masse to the days of small shops and single-family farms;
those options are no longer economically viable on any large
scale. Nor can we simply quit our jobs or abandon our

children. Broadening the awareness and sensitivity of employers to the problems fathers face and demanding and getting flexible work schedules, realistic paternity leave, and child-care policies will take considerable time and effort.

> *I really don't understand how the hell we are supposed to do this. It's like first we sat down and decided how we wanted to live our lives, and then we turned around and structured the real world in such a way that it would be impossible. My neighbor just got laid off, and he is such a wreck that his kids are tiptoeing around to avoid him. My company is doing so well that we are all putting in mandatory overtime, so I never get to see my kids.*

For all the world, it feels very much like we are stuck between a rock and a hard place, being slowly ground into pieces. And recent changes in our economic landscape are not making things any easier. The growing pains of a truly international economy have forced a wave of corporate downsizing, which in real language means that fewer good jobs are available; and the lucky ones who have those jobs are being increasingly called upon to work longer hours. As fathers, we have to fight in an intensely stressful job market to find work that will enable us to provide for our children; and, at the same time, if we are successful, we must somehow resist the job pressures that pull us farther and farther away from them.

Given all these factors, being a father at this moment in

history is no picnic. We are understandably expected to provide for our children, and attacked as deadbeat dads if we fail. At the same time, we end up sacrificing precious time with our children in order to provide for them, and then come under criticism for not being with them enough.

For many men, it feels like an impossible situation—and there are no easy fixes on the horizon. Yet this is the hand we have been dealt, and the stakes are far too high to walk away without trying. For, as great a social tragedy as the absent father has become, it is so much more a personal tragedy for our children, who are growing up without our support and nurturing, and for those of us who are severed from the miracle of our children's lives.

We need to begin to redefine fathering in a way that makes sense at this point in our history so that it can provide the kind of reassuring comfort and strength for our children that it should. We need to search for ways around the seemingly impossible binds we find ourselves in, so that when we work, it is for a deeper purpose that can be achieved, and when we are home with our children, it is as the fathers we want to be. In order to be able to do all this, we need to look a little closer at the more personal factors that keep us separated from our children.

Chapter 3

Outside from the Beginning

I thought I knew what I was getting into. I really did. I grew up in the sixties, and most of my friends were in no hurry to have children. But almost for as long as I can remember, I had loved kids and couldn't wait to have my own. When my wife got pregnant, I read everything about parenting I could get my hands on. I'm probably the only person in America to have actually read Dr. Spock cover to cover.

We were among the first wave of parents insisting on natural childbirth back when only a handful of hospitals allowed fathers into the delivery room. We even briefly considered something called the "LeBoyer method," which involved everyone speaking in whis-

*pers in a delivery room heated to body temperature
and then immediately submerging the new child in a
tub of 98.6° water. The idea was to make her transition from the relatively quiet and very warm, wet
world into the noisy, cold atmosphere of a standard
delivery room that much less traumatic.*

*I was totally into being a father and thought I was
prepared—until moments after my daughter's messy
arrival, when the nurse put this tiny little girl into my
hands. I was so overwhelmed by the flood of feelings
that I damn near dropped her. At that moment, the
only clear thought I had was sheer disbelief at how I
could ever have been stupid enough to think I was
ready for this.*

*I was scared. I was scared I would drop her, I was
scared something might happen to her, I was scared I
wouldn't be able to provide everything she deserved, I
was scared I would look scared when now more than
ever it seemed I had to be strong and in control, and
I was scared to death of how quickly and how deeply
I loved this squirming little girl.*

Fathers are different from mothers. It's so obvious that we
don't even stop to think about what the difference really
means. The relationship of a mother and her child develops
quite literally from the inside out. For nine months, the
mother and her child are together in a physical symbiosis
that defies comprehension. On the most elemental level,
they share in the miracle of creation, and the day of birth is

but the first important milestone in their already established connection.

Fathers, on the other hand, come to their children from the outside from the very beginning. We can participate in the progress of our wife's pregnancy, we can place our hands in strategic spots to feel the kicks and jabs, we can listen to the swooshing heartbeat through a stethoscope, and now, thanks to the marvels of technology, we can watch videos of our child floating gently within her embryonic world. But our experience is always filtered; no matter how we participate, fundamentally we remain on the outside. Our first real contact with our child is when we pick up our newborn and cradle her in our arms.

In some profound way, our biological placement in the process of birth mirrors the challenges we will face throughout our children's lives. For most mothers, the primary struggle of parenthood is stepping back far enough to allow the child the room to grow and develop. The challenge for most men, on the other hand, is coming in close enough so that we can build a strong and lasting bond.

As surprising as it might seem, the most crucial time to dramatically impact your future relationship with your children is in the first few years of their lives. This is a time when love and commitment are communicated on the most basic level. A child's infancy is a time of tremendous leverage. The foundation we establish—or fail to establish—will either allow us to build and maintain a close emotional connection with relative ease, or will instill a distance that will make our later efforts more difficult.

The birth of his first child is a pivotal moment in a father's life. It is a time when he must choose—whether he wants to or not—the emotional orbit from which he will do his fathering. The newborn offers a father an opportunity, a doorway back to the emotional world. This is an extraordinary, and tragically, often overlooked possibility. If we choose to open ourselves as widely as possible, to meet our child in the frighteningly vulnerable place from where they begin, it can reunite us with a time and place when we, too, felt completely defenseless, completely exposed, and completely vulnerable. In this manner, it can broaden us and make us wiser.

Pulled together at the moment of birth, father and child will either forge an unbreakable connection or begin drifting apart. This opportunity is fragile and fleeting, existing for only a brief moment before the mundaneness of daily life returns in full force. Once this time has passed, crossing the distance becomes more and more difficult. It can be done—distance can always be erased where the love and desire is strong enough—but it becomes more and more difficult as time passes.

Because of this, becoming a father is a precious and sacred time in a man's life but, unfortunately, it is rarely acknowledged as such. We arrive at this moment almost completely unprepared—no wise, elderly male relative takes us aside and impresses upon us the importance of seizing the chance for deep bonding. Too often, the moment passes without our even understanding the opportunity that is already slipping away.

When I think about it, I realize that I really didn't think a lot about what it would be like to actually be a father. Saying that now sounds absolutely idiotic, but I was really focused on my wife. Her pregnancy had been rough—nonstop morning sickness, daily afternoon headaches, and constant back pain and nausea the last two months. I was just trying alternately to comfort her, get some work done, and stay the hell out of her way.

When my son was born and the nurse asked me if I wanted to hold him, I realized that I didn't even know how. I couldn't figure out where to put the head or how to fit those tiny body parts into my very large and awkward-feeling hands. I also couldn't figure out how I ended up standing there so completely unprepared.

Fathering is one of men's most important and certainly most difficult undertakings, yet most of us enter into fatherhood with only the most rudimentary concept of what is expected of us. From any rational perspective, fatherhood is a great mystery. We live in a society that prizes preparation, training, and expertise for almost everything, but leaves us woefully unprepared for the single most challenging task of all. The more information we have, the more clear it becomes how vitally important the father/child relationship is, yet the patterns of our society appear to simply assume that men have but a ceremonial role in the shaping of their children's lives. We become fathers with stunning ignorance, and unfortunately the period of greatest nescience is the one we are smack in the middle of before we ever realize how ill-prepared we are: our child's infancy.

How come nobody warned us? Although in most cases our initiation into the bewildering world of fatherhood was not something done to us intentionally, at the time it certainly seems like a peculiarly cruel joke.

> One day shortly after my daughter was born, my wife was dead asleep and I was trying real hard to do my part. After ruining two diapers and finally managing to get the third to sort of hang around my baby's hips, I just started laughing. I couldn't believe I could be so inept. I don't remember even having seen a baby being diapered. Babies were always fully diapered; when they needed changing, they were whisked away only to reappear in full plastic armor. I came up with the theory that all the women in the world got together and agreed to not let little boys in on any of the secret stuff about babies.

For the most part, as boys we were rarely included in any infant-care activities and were unwelcome when adults talked about parenting issues. When a little brother or sister came along, we might have been ceremonially placed on a well-cushioned chair and allowed to "hold" him for a few minutes, but for all practical purposes, the message that came through loud and clear was that when Mom (occasionally with the assistance of Big Sister) was dealing with the babies, the best all-around strategy was for us to be some-where else—preferably harmlessly entertaining ourselves.

Nor did many of us have any real models for what a father is supposed to be. Our fathers, all too often, were not around. Either they were at work all day and sometimes until well into the evening (so they were too tired when they were home to really interact), or they were not even in the same household. And when they were around, they were generally uninvolved in the down-and-dirty parenting tasks. How many of us over the age of twenty-five can remember our fathers doing laundry or picking us up from school? On the day-to-day level, most of us grew up in a world where the nuts-and-bolts of parenting was done by women. Our chins and bottoms were wiped, our food prepared and served, and our scratches and bruises attended to and kissed away—mainly by Mom, but often with help from Grandma, a handful of aunts, and occasionally a big sister.

Our experience of fathering was usually restricted to predictably narrow areas: Dad firmly held the expectations that you were supposed to live up to; Dad lowered the boom when you really screwed up and was the one you went to when you had a big problem that needed solving; and every now and then he was the one who would take you on a special outing.

Given this cultural background, it is certainly under-standable that we would arrive at the gates of fatherhood woefully unprepared. What is difficult to understand is how, as a society, we could somehow silently conspire to bring one man after another to the brink of the most important job in his lifetime not only without preparing him, but without even talking to him about it.

> *My wife tells me there is nothing subtle about me, including my dreams. The day after my son was born, I had this dream where I am at a Dodger's baseball game and sitting in box seats right on the third-base line. The pitcher has gotten into trouble, and the pitching coach comes over to my box seats and says, "You're going in for him." The whole stadium is looking at me and waiting for me to get my butt to the mound so the game can resume, and I am glued to my seat in terror.*

When it comes to small children, this father's dream is all too often a reality; however, in the world of work this profound lack of preparation never happens. Imagine for a minute being relatively young and a pretty good salesman, though still fairly inexperienced in the working world, and the president of your multinational corporation calls you up to tell you that you've just been promoted to chief financial officer. After a momentary fleeting fantasy of the big raise and leap in status, you would no doubt conclude that this guy was nuts. You were no more prepared to be chief financial officer than you were to do the brain surgery your boss obviously needed!

We have dedicated the vast resources of our education system to prepare us for the tasks we will face later in life, but not only do we not teach our sons the skills they will need to be good fathers, we act as though fathering skills are instinctive or biological, and will simply emerge automatically, like a new mother's breast milk.

It doesn't work that way. When an infant cries, nursing mothers often experience a responsive leaking of breast milk; there are, after all, some powerful survival-of-the-species factors at work in that relationship. Unfortunately, a father does not automatically know what is wrong or what needs to be done when a baby cries. Fathering is a skill that must be learned and, for the most part, is one we don't bother to pass on.

Men also don't have the ritual support that so many women do. When a baby is born, grandmothers, sisters, and female friends all come out of the woodwork to hover and coo over the new addition, while the exhausted mom is alternately encouraged into her new child-care duties and pampered and fussed over by the temporary support team. It is a momentous occasion to cross over that unspoken borderline between being one of the women to being one of the mothers. It is observed and acknowledged in hundreds of small ways, from baby showers to visits from all the female relatives. It is not as though anyone decided or intended to exclude the new father, but the focus is clearly and specifically on mother and child—Dad is somewhere unobtrusively in the background.

The minute a man faces the most momentous change he will ever encounter, he is pressed by tradition, by circumstances, and often by his own fear into assuming a quietly receding position.

While reason and compassion dictate that the new father should be ritually welcomed and as emotionally propped up and supported at this crucial juncture as the new mother is, he is often ignored, left to deal with his insecurities with stoic silence or nervous bravado.

Even if men are properly prepared in the diaper-and-bottle department, we are still woefully unready for the sudden and dramatic realization of the awesome responsibility we have just taken on. You can do what you can ahead of time to prepare yourself, but nothing will make you ready for the impact of the feelings that are suddenly unleashed. This is your child, and it is your responsibility to protect her, to make sure that nothing bad ever befalls him.

The first time I had a chance to even stop and think about what had happened to me was about three months after my daughter's birth. I felt like I had been hit by a runaway truck and dragged for a mile. I never thought that my feelings of love would be so strong. I never realized that such a tiny little thing could so completely drain my energy. I never believed the comfortable routine I had built up with my wife and buddies could be so totally shattered. And I never could have imagined how frightening the weight of responsibility would be.

If there is any instinctive "father response" bred into men, most fathers would probably conclude that it is the overpowering urge to protect, at all costs, the helpless infant that has suddenly become their charge. It is a rare father who has not experienced that powerful rush of adrenaline at the door to fatherhood, and the strength of those feelings raises the odds dramatically. What prior to your first child's birth was a logical understanding of the extra financial burden you were about to undertake, coupled with a vague notion of the time and energy commitment that would be required, is suddenly elevated to life-and-death issues—this is your child, and your sense of duty and responsibility expands almost beyond bearing.

Ironically, men's response to this protective impulse often leads us into a series of actions and reactions that draws us farther and farther away from the real tasks of fathering. Becoming a father is almost always frightening, and, when our sensitivities are raised so quickly and dramatically at the birth of our first child, often our initial response is near-panic. Right when the arrival of our child has opened up emotional channels into the most vulnerable part of our heart, we are suddenly placed in a situation in which we don't understand the procedures, much less the rules, and we are hit with a very real and practical expansion of our job description.

Add to that a wife who is, at the very least, temporarily out of the job market, and you have a prescription for a large sack of emotional and financial burdens that men often find hard to carry. But carry it we must, because it is our job, because we feel it is our responsibility as men, even if we are not at all sure we can measure up. It can be a terrifying beginning, because if we can't protect our new family from even the insecurity caused by its inception, we will have failed before we've even begun. In the midst of this swirl of fear, our immediate response is to grab hold of anything that appears solid, and more often than not, that means putting up at least a pretense of being strong. We want our wives and babies to feel our protective strength, not our quivering insecurity. And often, that's what our wives want from us, too.

> *I remember lying on the bed with my wife just before our baby was born six years ago and telling her how afraid I was of not being a good father, of not being a good provider. She absolutely freaked out. "You can't be afraid!" she screamed. "I'm the one who's scared." I learned then to keep my mouth shut.*

Given all these realities, a new father can end up, not by design but by circumstance, withdrawing at precisely the moment he should be reaching out. Feeling unimportant, left out, and scared, he is apt to retreat into silent stoicism— feeling the enormous load of his newborn responsibility, but having no apparent support or acknowledgment from the outside and no ready avenue to relieve his burden.

> *It was really frightening. My wife was so wrapped up in the baby that it never occurred to her that we were going to have a very difficult time making it on my salary. My daughter was so beautiful, I used to stand at her crib late at night, watching her. Half the time*

my heart was full to bursting with love and the other half I was fighting down bile at the sheer terror of the responsibility I had taken on.

This terror of the burden we have assumed is often just the first subtle push of what, all too easily, can propel the new father into a trajectory that takes him away from his child. By shutting down instead of opening up, by pulling away toward the seductive safety of isolation instead of stepping forward into the frightening no-man's-land of an infant's very raw needs, a new father can unintentionally establish an emotional distance between himself and his child that will be difficult to bridge.

As I watched my wife breast-feeding our son, they seemed to be surrounded by some kind of beautiful, glowing light. It took my breath away, but it also made me feel so inadequate and so much like an outsider. I just thought the best thing I could do was to avoid disturbing them.

To some new fathers, witnessing the power of the mother/ child connection can be so dramatic that they retreat out of respect rather than fear. Add to that the return these days to breast-feeding rather than bottle feeding, and men can find themselves in the very uncomfortable position of not being able to satisfy their crying baby's very real need. Whether out of respect, fear, or circumstance, the result is the same—the entrenchment of distance between father and child.

> *It was like there was some kind of unspoken language*
> *that no one ever taught me. She was such a tiny thing,*
> *and her very survival depended on someone under-*
> *standing what she needed and providing it. At the*
> *time, I thought it must have been some magical*
> *genetic thing, because my wife—who frankly was never*
> *the most practical person in the world—suddenly*
> *seemed to understand exactly what this little creature*
> *needed. It wasn't until many years later that she told*
> *me how scared and inept she had felt.*

Ironically, our collective mythology about women being intuitive and "natural born" mothers often contributes to nudging new fathers away from forming a strong emotional bond with their newborn children early on. Many new mothers express their own insecurities about mothering by being overly attentive and focused on their infant. This can come across to an often nervous and baffled father as a possessive and near exclusive takeover of all the nurturing and comforting roles. We men frequently contribute to this unconscious takeover because, after all, we are already feeling inept, and it suits our need for security to imagine that our wives really are "naturally" good at this sort of thing.

Mom takes maternity leave and spends her time in intensive training sessions. Fathers, on the other hand, rarely take parental leave and begin almost immediately to see and interact with their child in limited and repetitive ways. As a result, the new mother quickly learns to interpret the cries and body language of her tiny infant. She becomes, through trial and error, in tune with the feelings and expressions of this emerging little person, while Dad lags behind. When Dad is late in picking up the infant's signs of need, Mom, who by now understands the signals, steps in to take over. Because children, like adults, naturally gravitate toward those who provide them with the nurturance and comfort they need, before we know what has happened, our babies are crawling to Mommy for comfort, our toddlers always want to go with Mommy—and we're left wondering what happened. The cumulative effect is the establishment of a polarization where Mom assumes virtually all the roles of comforting and nurturing, and Dad recedes into the distance—outside the orbit of the deepest emotional connections.

Just before my daughter's birth, my wife confessed that she was scared because she didn't feel like she knew how to be a mother. I did my best to console her and assure her that together we'd do just fine. Four months later she's slinging our daughter around like this is old stuff, and I come home from work feeling like the kid who fell off the wagon and is running like mad to catch up.

At the same time we are losing out on precious opportunities to bond with our baby, the first days of fatherhood are often taken up by myriad burdensome tasks, interrupted constantly. Whatever schedule we used to observe is blown to pieces. Waking, sleeping, eating, even limited conversation with your wife is now suddenly and completely at the unconscious whim of your child. Most men find themselves in the position of trying to smooth over all the interactions with the outside world, leaving mother and child within a hastily (and imperfectly) fashioned cocoon of protection.

Usually, this means that the careful division of labor you and your wife had become comfortable with is shattered by the unbelievable level of attention a newborn requires. While Mom redirects her energy toward caring for your child, you find yourself picking up the slack at the grocery store, in trips to the cleaners, in kitchen duty, and in any number of small but time-consuming tasks that must get done.

It is an exhausting time, made even more so by the predictable late-night alarm clock of your hungry child's cry. If the fatigue is being balanced by the emergence of deep emotional bonds between you and your child, it is only of passing consequence. But if the exhaustion is experienced only as the result of a very difficult job, as is so often the case with new fathers, the consequences can be lasting and tragic.

The first few months were such a whirlwind. Looking back, it just seems like a blur of exhaustion and stress. I can remember waking up in the middle of the night in terror that my daughter had stopped breathing. I don't even want to think about how many times I leaned into her crib to make sure she was breathing. My wife was totally absorbed. I felt like either the unnecessary third wheel or a reliable pack mule, putting one hoof in front of the other. When her three months of maternity leave were coming to an end, my wife announced that she had decided that she didn't want to go back to work, but wanted to stay at home and take care of our child.

Thinking back, it was really weird. I completely understood, I even completely agreed, yet at the same time I was hurt, angry, and scared—and I never said a word.

One day we are living lives that we can trace with some thread of consistency. The next day everything has changed so much we are mystified at how it happened. Somehow the boundaries of our existence have expanded dramatically. We can feel the enormity of the transformation, but we have no reference for understanding it nor anyone to talk to about it.

Indeed, for most us the transition to fatherhood is like being dunked into a bath of ice water: One moment we are young men concerned largely with our wife, our career, and our leisure time; the next moment we are fathers—not at all sure about what we are supposed to do but with a very definite sense that the scope of our responsibility has just increased enormously.

One of the secrets about good fathering is that it is primarily about feelings. His child's infancy is the time in a man's life when he is given the opportunity to return, fully and completely, to his heart. After spending much of the previous two or three decades learning how to conquer and control our feelings in order to operate effectively in the world, fatherhood presents us with the sudden and scary opportunity to become reacquainted with that inner part of ourselves.

My son was a very colicky baby. We went through nearly three months of sleepless, crying-filled days and nights. What I did not know then was what an amazing gift that would turn out to be. I quickly discovered that the most effective way to ease his discomfort was to hold him tightly against my chest and walk up and down the living room. It became an almost automatic routine: he'd cry; I'd pick him up press him to my body and begin pacing. Finally his little head would relax on my shoulder and I could feel the tension drain from his body.

I must have walked more than a hundred miles in our living room like that. One Sunday, I was pacing around in front of the television, giving him a running commentary on the football game I was watching and I realized that he was looking at me and giggling. His colic was completely gone, and the look on his face was this delightful knowledge that he had maneuvered me into this position of physical intimacy that I probably would not have had the brains or the courage to attempt if it weren't for my concern over his discomfort.

Life has a way of delivering lessons in a form that we can handle. Reintroducing a man to his emotional side can, as most women will certainly attest, be a very tall order. But when the teacher is his very own tiny, helpless infant, the process can be simple, painless, and a source of immeasurable joy, as many of the men I spoke with can attest. Cradled in the security of mutual, unconditional love, it is the single safest emotional relationship most men will ever encounter.

Interacting with an infant is the most introductory course in deep emotions imaginable. Add to that the fact that we are starting with the real basics—infants need to be held, fed, stroked, talked to, played with, bathed, and comforted—and you get to practice all you want without fear of rejection. You know going in that every touch, every funny face, every hug, every tickle, every time you tell him how much you love him, every time you watch her latest accomplishment with wonder, your child is blossoming with your love.

A child's infancy is a very physical time, so dive in and enjoy it. From feeding, diapering, and bathing to tying on those tiny booties and trying to direct a flailing hand down a shirt sleeve, it is a time when your child needs you to perform the most rudimentary and essential tasks. Despite the traditional gender allocation of these duties—with the single exception of breast-feeding—they are neither particularly mysterious nor difficult, and fathers aren't any less suited to them than mothers are. And they present us with daily opportunities to nurture and strengthen the bonds with our children.

I must have had the cleanest babies in the country. I started giving my first child a nightly bath very early and kept it up long after I realized she didn't really need a bath every night, simply because it was such a special time for both of us. I remember one time when she was around four or five months and she had discovered that she had some control over where her hands went. She spent the entire bath trying to slap the water. With a look of great concentration, she was moving her hand all over the place and completely ignoring me as I soaped her up and rinsed her off. When she finally succeeded—dousing me in the process—she looked at me with an expression that managed to combine complete wonder with bursting pride, and I laughed so hard her mother came running in to see what had happened.

Infancy is truly a time of miracles. Your child's mind and body are growing at such a dramatic rate that he is a new person every day. The tiny hand that waves aimlessly around one day is purposefully (and gleefully) dropping peas off the high chair tray the next. Overnight, all the gurgling and lip-smacking turn into distinct sounds, then words, then demands. The helpless, wiggling infant, whose sole method of getting anything accomplished is to cry, transforms before your very eyes (and long before you are properly prepared) into a marvel of locomotion, knocking down anything and everything in her path and turning any bottom shelf into complete disarray.

Babyhood may appear to be a period of great fragility, but in fact it's a rough-and-tumble time of constant creation and discovery. No father worth his salt would allow his child to disappear on a long journey of exploration unaccompanied, which is exactly what happens if you don't make an conscious effort to dive into fatherhood—by becoming a master of the quick diaper change, learning the intricate flight patterns for spooning mashed peas into an anxiously circling mouth while enthusiastically babbling nonsense, locating every ticklish spot on your child's body, and reading *A Fly Went By* seven hundred times without appearing to lose interest in how it will turn out.

Isn't it odd how you can go through years of living on automatic pilot—not thinking, not feeling, just blindly following some script someone handed you long, long ago. When my son was born, for all practical purposes I was not involved. I was out of town the day he arrived, and I was at the office throughout most of his first three years. By the time I really started to wake up, he was a very angry four-year-old, not at all sure he wanted anything to do with me. Here I am, seventeen years later, and it is still a very painful process.

I was determined not to make the same mistakes with my daughter. I spent as much time as I could with her; I was even the first man in my company to take paternity leave. What I was totally unprepared for was how profoundly the experience of being there with her would affect me. I have always prided myself on being very rational and articulate, and this little-bitty person without a vocabulary to speak of turned my life upside down in ways I will never be able to repay.

As new fathers, we enter this moment of our lives profoundly unprepared. If we have a supportive wife, if we can find the courage to overcome our fears and insecurities, if we are lucky enough to have male friends to encourage us in the process, we have the opportunity to begin again—to actively participate in the miraculous process of creating an individual. And in so doing, we are taken back and allowed to relive, re-create, and refashion those parts of our own being that no longer serve us well.

It seems important to start with this, the deepest truth of fathering—that your children can take you back and can set you free. From here we can begin to create the intricate web of connections that bind us to our children. It is never too early to begin but, because of the miracle of love, it is also never too late.

Chapter 4

The Heart of Fathering

Over the past forty-six years, I've learned almost nothing about expressing my feelings to others. It's not that I don't want to. I try to be available to help out my kids when they need me, but beyond that I have no idea what I should do to let them know how much I feel for them. It's easier to let them come to me if they need something, because I have a hard time figuring out how to initiate any meaningful conversation.

If we are failing our children, it is not because we don't love them, not because we don't want to be the best father we can possibly be, but rather because the rules have all changed and no one bothered to tell us, much less give us a copy of the new rule book. We feel, as one man said, "a little like a character in a *Twilight Zone* episode. One day I just woke up in another dimension, where no matter what I tried to do, it turned out to be the wrong thing."

At the heart of the problem is our collective difficulty in dealing with things emotional, an inhibition that robs our children of one of the most essential resources necessary for building a healthy, self-confident personality: our heartfelt, feeling presence.

Under normal circumstances, our strength as problem solvers would rise to the occasion. However, growing up male has ill-prepared us for dealing with this one—we have a very limited emotional vocabulary and little experience, much of it negative, in emotional dialogue. It is one of the problems that helped get us here in the first place. Often we remain at arm's length from our children, because we fear we don't have the skills to do it right. We inherited this lack of emotional facility from our fathers, who themselves struggled mightily in the emotional realm.

My father is a very quiet man. He never calls me on the phone and hardly says two sentences when we are together. When I was growing up, he and I went through some pretty rugged times, but he was always there when I needed him. I remember the day I told him my wife and I were getting a divorce. I was scared to death to tell him. I was already an emotional wreck and was terrified he would disapprove and lecture me. Instead, he said that the world I was living in was so different from his that he had no idea what he would have done in my place. Then he told me he would love and support me no matter what I did.

I thought that conversation was about as emotional as my father could get, until just last year. He came over to see me on a Saturday, very agitated. He'd been listening to a talk radio program about fathers, and a number of callers had been complaining about how much it had hurt that their fathers never told them they loved them.

I can remember at least three times my father told me he loved me, but he couldn't remember and was worried that he had really blown it. There we were in the garage, me trying to finish some dollhouse furniture I had promised my daughter, and him trying to figure out how to say "I love you." It took him nearly an hour, and I think it was the hardest thing he ever did in his life.

Because we, too, for the most part were raised to follow a similar code of emotional silence, we find ourselves untrained, unsupported, unsure, and uneasy in the crucial task of emotionally nurturing our children. But this is precisely what we are being called upon to do.

It is always difficult to make a change, because it's new, because it's different, but mostly because it implies that the way we used to do it was all wrong. In practice, things don't really work that way. What was appropriate forty years ago may not be appropriate today. Largely because we have had virtually no training for what is being asked of us, this particular transition for men is even more difficult and confusing than most. The temptation is to long for the illusory comfort of some past golden era. But fathering is too important to treat so cavalierly. We must face who we are and where we are right now. Like it or not, whereas our fathers pioneered a new technological era, we now blaze a trail on the frontier of human relationships.

There is a scene in one of the *Star Trek* movies in which Captain Kirk says: "The situation is grim and the odds of succeeding are slim—sounds like fun." It's poking fun at the swashbuckling nature of the early *Star Trek* TV show, but it's also speaking to the fearless adventurer within each of us. Historically, when fathers were called upon to be protectors, it was in deadly serious physical combat. Whether it was battling a marauding group of bandits, a rival tribe, or an organized army of invaders, they fought to protect their children.

This is a characteristic of fathering that we are comfortable with; it is the most visible and receives the most attention—that of protector. Along with the ability to solve problems and resolve conflicts, a father's role as protector is something we as a society have traditionally appreciated; it is perhaps the most dramatic manifestation of father love.

But in the final analysis, the most important quality of a good father at this point in history is the capacity to communicate and share deep feelings with our children. That's because the heart of fathering is fathering from the heart. It is about how our children feel, about us, about their own self-esteem and sense of self-worth, about the value and importance of their unique personalities. It is about how effective we are at helping our children understand and embrace their own feelings. These are the most precious gifts that we can give our children, the resources that will allow them to successfully live rich and full lives.

Although fathering on the day-to-day level is often about *doing*—something for which most of our fathers prepared us very well—on the fundamental level it is almost exclusively about *feeling*. This crucial truth is easy for us to dismiss or ignore.

Because it seems to come more naturally to us and because we are better at it, we tend to elevate the role of father as teacher to a position of highest importance. We focus on the need to teach our children good, effective behavior so that whatever they do in life they will do well.

As men we tend to define ourselves by the work we do. I am a carpenter, a lawyer, a manager, a mechanic. But obviously we are much more than that. We are fathers, husbands, lovers, sons; we are members of a broader community; we are individuals with our own beliefs and convictions. Ultimately, when we really want someone to understand our uniquely individual perspective, we say, "I *feel* very strongly about this."

I had been having real problems with my daughter; she was angry, rebellious, and surly, and I didn't understand why. Finally, a friend of mine took me aside and told me to stop responding to what she said

*and try instead to respond to how she felt. I admit, I
didn't really understand what she meant, but a few
days later my daughter and I got into it again. It
started over some fight she had with her best friend,
and I made some pretty neutral remark and then she
went nuts. I thought about it and figured I had
nothing to lose, so I went into her room and said
something like, "It must feel pretty lousy having your
best friend desert you like that." I'm sure it came out
much less articulate than that, but it was like magic.
She threw herself into my very surprised arms and
burst into tears, and the next thing I knew I was so
choked up I could hardly speak.*

Once again, we are being called to fight for our children,
only this time the battle is in a decidedly different arena and
will not be waged with muscle and weapons. We can draw on
the courage and determination of the generations of fathers
that have gone before us, but we must develop new and
different skills. This time the enemy is all the nameless and
faceless pressures that push us away from a deep connection
with our children. Our battle is about feelings—ours and
theirs. Ultimately, it is about becoming conversant enough
and comfortable enough with our own emotions to be able
to receive and nurture the feelings of our children.

This, then, is our challenge: to become emotional war-
riors, to return to the heart of fathering. We must approach
this challenge with determination and the conviction that
by focusing our efforts here, at the very core of what it means

to be a father, we can rewrite the rules and transform the landscape of parenting.

I couldn't believe it. We were sitting in a coffee shop, I was about to get into my car and drive two hundred miles to a new job, and they were looking at me with this scared, hurt expression. I wanted to tell them how much I loved them, I wanted to reassure them that I would always be there in their lives, but at first I just couldn't get the words out of my mouth. And then I just decided I was not leaving that stupid booth until I had told them what I needed to tell them. When I finally found the words, they came out in a frog-like voice, but the look on their faces made it worth it.

Communicating our love to our children and acknowledging their importance in our life is an undertaking of enormous significance, for our children, for our own well-being, and for generations of fathers yet to come. Historically and socially, we are conditioned to be able to put aside our feelings in order to fight. Now the purpose for which we must fight is to become fully engaged with our feelings in order to reinstate ourselves in our proper place in our children's lives. The effort requires courage and determination, for this is new territory, an area in which we will no doubt make mistakes.

It is also an endeavor that still, despite the pioneering work of many fathers, runs counter to what is expected and accepted. "Out there," in the world, the business culture still expects us to exist primarily for the sake of doing our job. The man who is perceived as being more concerned about spending time with his children than worrying about his job is still looked down on by many as ineffectual or, more bluntly, as a wimp.

I wanted to be really involved in my child's upbringing, but I have to admit that taking time off to care for him when he was small was a mixed bag. One day I was out walking him in his stroller and I heard a couple of businessmen walking by make some snide comment. It made me feel ashamed, like I wasn't really a man. You put all this effort into figuring out exactly how you want to live your life, but it is still awful hard to tune out the very songs you were raised to dance to.

There is a subculture in the working world made up of men who have chosen to sacrifice any and all genuine human interactions for the sake of business success. Many in this group rise to important positions precisely because they are willing to sacrifice everything, including their relationship to their wife and children, to succeed. Unfortunately, these are sometimes the very people the rest of us must somehow deal with; and all too often the only way they know to defend their own choices is to be absolutely cutthroat in their dealings regarding any man unwilling to make the same sacrifices.

Make no mistake, this is and will continue to be a substantial obstacle. For a man who has chosen to sacrifice family life for the sake of his job to see another man refuse to make that sacrifice and still be an effective worker starkly reveals the unnecessarily tragic folly of such a decision. Because of this, there will be plenty of men out there who will go out of their way to make it more difficult for you.

I worked with this man who had no life whatsoever except for work. I mean, he was completely obsessed with who sat where, who appeared in what position in what company photographs. He'd be on the telephone at eleven o'clock at night, thinking he was just incredibly important. One evening I was getting ready to leave, and he was needling me about "commitment" and "dedication"; I told him about a quote I had read somewhere, something to the effect that on their death bed very few people ever complain that they wished they had spent more time at the office. I meant it, but I probably should not have said anything, because he never forgot it and for years he did everything he could possibly do to make my life hell.

It takes considerable courage to walk through that wall of fire with the commitment to being a feeling man intact. Even in the best of work environments, it is rare that a man will find true support of career sacrifices made in the name of good fathering.

One of the reasons I went to work for this company was because they had a good parental-leave policy, but when it came right down to it, it was really tough. My boss came right out and told me not to do it—that I was needed. He never threatened me explicitly, but it was certainly implied.

In some senses, the external obstacles we must be prepared for will be the easiest to deal with. They are at least easy to identify, and we can fall back on our more familiar male problem-solving skills to get around them. The internal obstacles are more difficult both to pin down and to deal with.

One of the thorniest issues stems from the sad truth that in today's world, men do not get status for being good fathers, but rather for making lots of money and wielding lots of power. We may deplore the heartless, superficial nature of this pecking order, but can we resist the sirens' call? Like those mythical beauties whose songs lured sailors onto the deadly rocks, the attraction of status will be tempting. Raised on the importance of competition and striving for excellence, can we refuse to compete in the arena? We know it is distorted and out of balance, but we also know that this is where the public rewards are being handed out.

This is a delicate issue. Working and achieving are important; they are necessary to being a good provider. And, if we are lucky, it can be through our work that we make a contribution and thus our mark in the world. The trick is to accomplish what we need to without crashing on the rocks of total self-absorption.

I had to learn the hard way that you can't be completely dedicated to the demands of your job without shortchanging your children. It was only when my daughter developed childhood leukemia that I got my head straight about what was really important. I cut way back on my work schedule, something I would never have considered two years ago, to spend as much time with her as I possible could. So far, work, she, and I are all still surviving.

For many of us, the most difficult obstacle to overcome will be our fear of our own emotions. In one of Western civilization's greatest speeches, Winston Churchill hardened the determination of the British to resist Hitler by reminding them that "we have nothing to fear but fear itself." For a man, that call to courage is much easier to rally to when the danger is from the outside. When the danger appears to well up within our own hearts, however, we are not at all sure we have the resources to persist.

Our cultural stereotypes portray women as too focused on emotions, and men as largely oblivious to the world of feelings.

The theme recurs with as much regularity in domestic quarrels as it does in bestselling books and comedy routines. That's because, as much as it is a gross overstatement, it is also substantially true.

If we as fathers are to make this journey, we must admit

up front how difficult it is for most of us to be willing to feel—
much less express—the full range of emotions we have so
successfully kept bottled up. After all, it's tough to become
a skilled practitioner at anything if you can't at least begin
with a clear picture of your own weaknesses.

A good part of the problem is of our own making. For a
world of reasons that psychologists would be more than
happy to explain, most of us developed quite early the habit
of avoiding our emotions by simply repressing them whenever they tried to well up. We'd shove them down into some
dark space, where we hoped they would stay—and they
would, for the time being. But emotions have their own
rhythm and cannot be ignored so easily, at least not perma-
nently. Eventually they come out—one way or another.

The net effect of tamping them down is much like
overinflating a tire: The ride gets more and more jarring, and
the pressure mounts to the point where you are cringing at
every bump in anticipation of a blowout. After years of
allowing the pressure to build, it can take considerable
courage just to be willing to acknowledge and examine the
feelings that have been bottled up for so long, and even more
courage to actually feel and express them.

> I've been through thick and thin. I've done things no
> sane person would even consider. I've been in knife
> fights, fire fights, and forest fires, and the hardest
> thing I have ever done was to face my son after twenty
> years of neglect and tell him how sorry I was.

Men tend to be pretty good at analysis, but it helps if what we are analyzing can be seen, touched, measured, and examined. Emotions are more like energy than anything else. Although we can see the effect, we can't see emotions themselves. They pulse, vibrate, and crackle like an overloaded transformer, but we cannot get our hands on them. We can sense their tremendous power, but it cannot be controlled or harnessed. Entering the world of our own emotions, therefore, can be every bit as frightening as the idea of holding ten thousand volts of electricity in our hands.

> *I think I did everything possible to avoid facing up to my own feelings, but I just kept coming back to the same place. Finally, it was like I had reached the very bottom and it didn't even matter anymore. It felt for all the world like as soon as I let those feelings in, I would be swept away on this irresistible tide of sadness, fear, pain, heartbreak, and terminal loneliness. I felt just like Humpty-Dumpty—that I would end up so completely shattered that they would never be able to put me back together again.*

Ironically, one of the miracles of our emotions is that they allow us to experience things vastly beyond the limited capacities of our physical self. Our emotions, our extraordinary capacity to feel, constitute the expansive energy that makes up our essential identity—the core of who we are. Everything we are flows from that source: what we want and need in life, our desires, our hopes, our dreams. In a very profound way, each of us is truly what we feel.

Once we are willing to enter this world without reservation, we discover (to our great relief) that as overwhelming as it can feel, it is only a feeling. Not only can we survive, we can thrive as we become more and more comfortable in this venue. And thankfully, because the world of our emotions is a vastly complex and intricate one of which we can no longer remain ignorant.

We need to become experts—to learn how to harness this extraordinary energy, how to understand what we are feeling, and why we are experiencing those particular feelings. We need to learn how to describe and communicate our feelings in a way that others can understand. These skills are critical because they are the tools with which we will build a strong and lasting connection to our children.

If we imagine our emotions as high-voltage electricity pulsing within us, all that is missing is the connection—the circuitry—that allows that energy to flow back and forth between us. Without this connection, we are like a power tool that is unplugged. We can be present physically, interacting with our children, but the powerful flow of our vital energy is missing—an emotional blackout. It's like trying to drill a hole with a disconnected power drill—something may be happening, but it won't be what you are trying to accomplish.

One of life's greatest mysteries is reconciling our existence as unique individuals with the reality that we are intricately connected to everyone and everything. We are, in fact, both alone *and* connected.

As men, we are intimately familiar with the first truth. Very early in life, we learn that we are on our own. We are schooled in isolation, we learn to accept it as a natural part of our existence, and we create a safe place inside ourselves to which we can retreat. From this place we can, if necessary, dismiss anything outside ourselves as unimportant. This ability of men to become islands unto ourselves is also what allows us to pursue our dreams, interests, our goals with dogged determination. We can strip away everything else and bear down on precisely what we want.

This capacity to retreat to a place of our most basic needs is a powerful survival tool, and as ruthless as it appears, it is very effective. Cross us, attack us, insult us, hurt us, and we can survive by retreating to this place, where nothing that the other person says or does is important. Unfortunately, although this skill can be very useful on the battlefield, it can be very destructive when employed with those we hold most dear.

I had really been under pressure at work (this is my way of trying to excuse the inexcusable), we were in the midst of some very sensitive negotiations, and on top of that, for purely personal reasons, I was being constantly undermined by a member of my own working team. I came home one day and my son started in on me about this car he wanted help buying. At one point he said "I think" something or other, and I just cut him off, saying, "I don't care what you think." I was so caught up in my own pressure cooker, I probably would not have even noticed if the effect hadn't been so dramatic. He stopped midword, got this unbelievably stricken look on his face, and ran, and I mean ran, out of the room. That's when I realized what I had said and how I had said it. I couldn't believe myself. Here was this beautiful, sensitive kid that I loved more than anything in the world, and I had just dismissed him like a piece of litter.

The second part of the paradox of aloneness and connection is what has always caused us trouble. For we are very good at retreating to our island, but we are not nearly so skilled at extending ourselves to others, building the bridge to someone else. It is an undertaking that requires great faith and courage, because the very act of acknowledging our connection forces us to drop our defenses and makes us vulnerable.

The currency of that connection is love, and for most men, our love for our children is the safest and most stable place to begin. It is love that gives us the courage and audacity to extend our hands to another. It is love that grants us the courage to open the door to our inner self and stand there, vulnerable and exposed in front of others.

It is in this space, the circuitry we create to bridge the gap between us, that we are able to share at the deepest level the most important aspects of who we are. And, it is in this connection that we are able to receive the miracle of our children's love.

God, I hate to admit this, but when I got married I truly believed that love was just a gushy myth we liked to tell ourselves. I thought you simply picked someone you liked, someone you could talk to and be friends with, and then settled down to raise a family. Then my daughter was born, and it was like somebody hit the color switch on an old black-and-white TV. It changed everything, totally and completely and irreversibly. I had never even imagined that the feelings that were coursing through my body could exist, much less exist on a constant, daily basis.

Very few things that we as men will ever experience are as deep and powerful as our love for our children. It is an extraordinarily primal, almost visceral feeling, and we don't always know how to react to it. For most of us, it is impossible to describe—we simply cannot find the words. Partly because of that, we resist talking about it. It resides inside us in a protected place, like a precious treasure that must be guarded.

Ironically, because we don't talk about it, the feeling itself becomes more powerful and mysterious, making us even more unwilling to discuss it. We're afraid that if we tried to talk about our love for our children, we would either stumble around, unable to find the proper words to convey the feeling, or, worse, that the sheer depth and power of the feeling would cause our voices to falter. Indeed, in many of the interviews I did for this book, voices cracked with emotion when fathers spoke about their love for their children.

Because it can be so overwhelming, too many of us assume that the mere existence of such a powerful feeling is sufficient for our children's well-being—but it isn't. That feeling, that unconditional love and commitment to our children, is the foundation of our future and the salvation of our past; but it is nothing unless and until we can bring it forth and offer it to our children in ways they can receive.

We are all alone and we are all connected, but it is the feeling of being alone that will remain with us until we learn how to fashion the lasting bonds that connect us. We cannot experience the richness of being a part of something larger than ourselves, nor can we offer our children the security of truly feeling that they are not alone, without first being willing to take the risks entailed in learning to embrace and articulate our emotions.

One day I came home very late to find my father sitting in the living room. All the lights were out and he was just sitting there. He looked so fragile and so alone. I asked him if he was all right, and he just looked at me and said, "I don't want to die having never been loved." It really shook me up. That stayed with me for a long time, until I finally promised myself that I would not end up that way. I would do anything, take any risk, I'd walk through a wall of fire if necessary, but I would not end up in a dark room, wondering what happened to my life.

This challenge cannot be avoided if we want to take our fathering seriously. For it is here, in the charged atmosphere of shared feelings, that we will truly meet our children. It is here in the articulation of our deepest feelings that we can weave the deep chords of strength that will sustain our children throughout their lives. And it is here, face to face with the unconditional love of our children, that we will receive the greatest of gifts.

Chapter 5

Accepting the Powerful Responsibility of Fathering

One day when my son was very young, he was playing some game, climbing all over me and whooping. I had a splitting headache and after asking him a few times to keep it down, I snapped and just screamed at him. He disappeared, and about an hour later, I went to check on him; he was sitting in the corner of his room with a look on his face like a frightened animal. God, did I ever feel like a heel.

The human mind is an extraordinarily facile instrument. We can make penetrating deductions, rigorously work our way through a vastly complicated analysis, and daringly invite insight in the wide-open space between what we know and what we believe. Yet it is so difficult for us to hold onto one of life's most basic truths: We all know from intimate experience that our fathers had an almost unbelievably powerful influence on our lives, yet it seems so difficult for us to remember that this is exactly the same power we wield over our own children.

The Japanese have a saying they use to help them remember; loosely translated, it says that the three awe-inspiring forces of nature are typhoon, earthquake, and father. From the vantage point of our small children, we must look very much like a force of nature, or at least like one of the mythical Greek gods. Along with their mothers, we tower over them, speak in what must sound like booming voices, have powers that they cannot begin to understand, seem to possess vast knowledge of everything under the sun, and are the source of all food, toys, and comfort. It does not matter that in reality we are very flawed mortals; what matters is how our children feel, and in their emotional experience, we are giants.

As Zeus, Hera, and the rest of the Olympian crew were well aware, having so much power over others carries with it an awesome responsibility, and the very first rule of the powerful is to never forget the power you have. This can be much harder than it seems. By time we become fathers, we have already spent most of our life in the other position—that of being a son. We have cringed at the slightest sign of Father's displeasure, worried over whether he would be disappointed at our efforts, basked in the glory of his attention, and tried in our own unique ways to be someone he could be proud of.

> *At Thanksgiving last year, we were all talking at the table after dinner, and I said something like, "Oh, shit . . . " My father stared at me just like he used to when, as a young boy, I did something he didn't approve of. It stopped me in my tracks. I'm thirty-six years old with two kids of my own, but every time my father is in the same room with me, I feel just like I did when I was a kid.*

We spent the first decade of our life virtually powerless, and a solid two decades (and often more) at the mercy of our father's extraordinary ability to affect us, either positively or negatively. The gap between the awesome power we felt our father to possess and the complete lack of power we experienced when we were young is so huge that we appear unable to step across it with any ease or consistency. We forget what it was like for us when we were young, and in the forgetting, can appear very much to our kids like a wild-eyed Zeus emerging from our sanctuary, tossing lightening bolts.

> *One summer we were at the beach, and I had just bought these expensive flippers and masks for my kids. I was pushing my daughter out on a paddle board so she could float around and see all the fish without having to worry about staying afloat, and before we even got out past the breakers, she had lost one of her*

flippers. I yelled at her and she started crying; I felt like
such a jerk. I realized that as much as I wanted her to
have a good time, she wanted to please me and I had
ruined it. She didn't deserve that.

The emotional responsibility we assume by becoming fathers goes well beyond avoiding the inadvertent trampling about. It is as often what we do *not* do and do *not* say that strikes with the force of a thunderclap.

Some things just stick with you no matter how much
you want to forget them. My mother died when I was
eight. My dad was devastated and he just shrank back
into a shell. All I can remember is hurting so bad I
thought I'd die from heartbreak and my father never
trying to comfort me; he never said a word about her
and wouldn't let me talk about her. It was like she had
never lived.

As fathers, even if we are at a place in our lives where we feel very small and unimportant, even if our sense of self-confidence and self-worth is hanging down around our socks, even then, everything we do and say, as well as all the things we forget to do or are unable to say, will leave deep impressions on our children. It is our responsibility to remember that, so the impact we have will add to our children's strength and not to their wounds.

> *I grew up in awe of my father, even though I rarely saw*
> *him. He worked nights, and during the day my mother*
> *was always telling us to be quiet so he could sleep. On*
> *the weekends, we were not to disturb him because that*
> *was his only time to relax. My mother used to try to*
> *include him in our family life by saying things like,*
> *"Your father loves you," or "Your father is very proud*
> *of your report card," but the truth is I never really*
> *knew him.*

We contribute to the problem by being uncomfortable in expressing our emotions, particularly the joyful, silly, giddy kind that our children are so good at evoking. The feelings rise up, we get twitchy and awkward, start to feel embarrassed, and then retreat or pull away, just to create enough space around us to feel comfortable again. But it is exactly that distance that convinces our children that we are in fact different than others, somehow larger than life.

Ultimately, however, there is very little we can do about the royal status bestowed upon us by our children. There is no point protesting and there is no way of escaping. Eventually, our children grow up and see that we possess the same flaws, blemishes, and weaknesses as the rest of the species. By then, much of the damage or benefits we might have bestowed from our lofty position has already been internalized.

In the meantime, it helps if we focus our attention on what we can do to exercise our power as responsibly as possible. One of the best things we can do is to speak softly, act gently, and make ourselves as much a part of their world as we can. Giants are much easier to deal with when there is clearly nothing to fear. Although *we* know that a sharp or impatient tone of voice is just the hangover from a lousy day at the office or a domestic disagreement, our kids don't. Our impatience can be amplified in their minds to raging anger, irritation can swell into fantasies of murderous rage, and busyness can be interpreted as a lack of caring.

We live in a different world than children do. Ours is populated by a strikingly homogeneous group of well-intentioned bumblers—we are all stumbling along life's highway, doing the best we can and screwing up on a somewhat regular basis. We may not love our mistakes, but we are very familiar with them and accept them as a normal and perhaps even useful part of the journey.

Our children's world, on the other hand, is in many ways like the mysterious world of fairy tales. Magic things happen, both the amazingly beautiful and the terrifyingly ugly. When you do not know why or how things happen, any explanation seems as reasonable as the next, and our children start off without any answers. Under the circumstances, it is no wonder these little people are such information sponges—they need answers, and quickly.

Add to this mix the charming and irritating fact that small children are also quite convinced that they are the center of the universe, and you can end up with some pretty wild results. It is actually quite astonishing, given their position of near complete powerlessness, that they are nonetheless capable of truly believing (or at least seriously worrying) that they have somehow caused everything from Dad's bad mood to a death or divorce in the family.

We thought we had explained everything as well as we could, but about five months after I had moved out, I was trying to go to the store, and my son was insisting that first he had to finish cleaning up his room. I thought that was pretty strange, coming from a kid who made a habit of living in chaos and who spent much of his first six years fighting like a pit bull over having to clean up his room. I went in to check on him, and he had this scared look on his face as he rushed around, trying to toss clothes back into the closet and toys into the toy box.

That night I talked to his mother, and she confirmed that our little Pig Pen had become Mr. Clean at her house as well. The next day, I sat him down and told him all over again that his mother and I were not living together because we had decided it wasn't right for us. That it had nothing to do with him or anything he had done or not done. I never thought I'd say this, but the next week when I found myself arguing with him over the mess in his room, I was secretly thrilled.

The bottom line is that we need to do all we can to diffuse these flights of grim fantasy, at the same time insisting that Dad is a mere mortal, but one quite capable of and committed to caring for and protecting them. In other words, we need to tell our children the true story—that we are just like them only we have grown up. We too were once small children with giantlike fathers of our own. Just like them we had to learn how to tie our shoes, we too spilled our milk, and we didn't always pick up our toys.

We need to tell these stories over and over again, and they are best delivered and understood when we are a consistent part of our children's lives—when we play with them, hold them, and talk about things that interest them. The more we can shrink ourselves to their size and communicate on their level, the harder it will be for their fertile minds to inflate us to dangerous proportions. The more absent we are, however, the more time they spend with fantasies rather than flesh-and-blood fathers.

My father died when I was two. My mother never remarried and she used to tell me all these stories about what a great guy he was. I guess without even thinking about it, I made him into some kind of saint in my mind, and I tried very hard to be worthy of being his son. Then one day when I was in high school, a kid was taunting me and called my dad a drunk. I went nuts and starting beating on this kid. I ended up in the vice-principal's office, and my mother was called down. I found out that my father was an alcoholic and had died, drunk, in an automobile accident. I just stopped caring, and it was nearly ten years before I started to care about anything or anyone again.

In telling our children the truth about ourselves, it is essential that we make them understand the heart of fathering—that our love for them simply *is*. It is not something that must be earned or can be lost. We may get angry sometimes, we may be upset or disappointed over some transgression or another, but always behind the emotion of the moment is the unstoppable fountain of our love.

This is one of the greatest mysteries of life. When our children arrive in this world—tiny, defenseless, and completely helpless—they possess a crucial survival skill: the ability to plant in our hearts a love so deep and lasting that it cannot be extinguished. With the possible exception of the instinct to suck, it may be the only thing they do well at first, but it is the most important. It is this foundation of unshakable love that our children rely on to build their lives: If my father loves me no matter what, I don't need to be or do anything to feel worthy of love. If my father loves me no matter what, I am free to make mistakes, to stumble and fall. If my father loves me no matter what, I can go to sleep each night feeling safe, knowing that tomorrow will unfold with boundless possibilities.

This power we have over our children, to bring them sorrow or joy, to help them flower into the fullness of their potential or wither from lack of attention, is an immense responsibility. From the moment our first child is born, we are no longer free to be children ourselves. It is an indelible moment of transition: the baton has been passed and, regardless of age or experience, we are now fathers and had better start acting like it. All the Peter Pan fantasies we might have engaged in, all the growing up we might have deftly avoided are no longer viable options. All the rules change with the birth of our first child.

In a heartbeat, we move from believing in Santa Claus, to wishing he were real, to *being* Santa Claus. It sometimes seems like just when we finally get to stop worrying about pleasing Dad, we suddenly realize that we *are* Dad.

I grew up in the sixties, and although Bill Clinton may not have inhaled, everyone else who grew up in those years did. When my wife got pregnant she stopped smoking, but I didn't. One night about a week after my daughter was born, I was smoking a joint in the living room when my daughter woke up with a burning-hot fever. It scared me to death. I was so stoned I couldn't have driven her to the hospital had it been necessary. It was at that moment I realized what having a child really meant.

The bottom line is that kids will be kids, so *we* can't be anymore. Not that we shouldn't jump at the wonderful opportunity to hone our capacity for play, but we no longer have the luxury of indulging in exuberant immaturity. Emotionally, we must grow up, because it is our job to provide a responsible safety zone for the emergence of these amazing, whirling, twirling, churning creatures that are our children.

We can't come home from a bad day at work and take it out on the kids with abrupt, surly comments. It's one thing to stomp around in front of our wife or lover, who has the maturity and resources to decide just how much sympathy to hand out before politely asking us to act our age; it is quite another to expose our children to this kind of display. They don't have the resources to understand why Dad is acting so oddly, and they shouldn't be put in that position in the first place.

My father used to fly into rages and hit me. As I child, I swore I would never treat my kids like that. But now that I am a father, I often find myself in the same position. Exhausted after a hard day at the office, I lose my temper and can feel my hand twitching to go up. But then I remember my promise to myself and use the occasion to count to ten.

As obvious a requirement of good fathering as it is, becoming emotionally responsible for our children is not always easy. To really do it right requires learning the fine art of finding and holding the middle ground. From too far a distance, we cannot always see clearly what is going on, whereas if we are too close, we can easily lose the necessary perspective.

Growing up, my father made the rules and we followed them. I wasn't about to get dragged into nonstop negotiations, so one night when my daughter insisted that I come get her because there was a monster under her bed, I yelled at her to go to sleep and assumed that was it. About half and hour later, I heard her crying and went in to tell her to go to sleep. Under her bed was this rat that had apparently eaten rat poison and was on its last legs. It really shook me up.

Sometimes finding the middle ground means moving in closer to get a better view of a situation, such as when we are trying to work at home and are interrupted by sounds of bedlam coming from our children's room. From our position, glued in earnest concentration to the computer, the most natural reaction might be a loud, bellowing demand for peace and quiet (Zeus tossing around a few thunderbolts). But if we rise from our throne and investigate the scene of the outburst, we can see much more clearly what the appropriate reaction should be. There might actually be something going on that requires our attention. It may just be out-of-control sibling warfare, but by moving closer to bring the true picture into focus *before* reacting, our response will be more informed, appropriate, and responsible.

Conversely, sometimes finding the middle ground requires stepping back. The best examples arise from what might charitably be called àrguments with our children. We can all too easily get dragged into conversations that would be downright embarrassing if captured on video: whining, demanding, "I always"s and "you never"s on their part; a host of shouting, criticizing, and "because I said so!"s on our side. At times like these, we need to step back, disengage, and get a little perspective on what is really going on.

I have no idea what was going on in my head, but there I was, sitting on the floor, arguing with my five year old over the rules to "Candy Land." I mean, I was upset because she was breaking rules right and left in order to win. In the middle of this pitched battle, my wife walked into the room, quickly sized up the situation, and innocently asked which one of us kids was winning.

What is usually going on is that our children are acting like children, which is to say, frequently straying outside the bounds of accepted civilized behavior. That is a natural and important part of growing up; it's *not* all right, however, for us to follow their lead. We need to remember that this is a big part of what childhood is all about—learning how to have meaningful, effective communication that conveys your point of view without decimating the other person, and how to behave in ways that are appropriate—that calling someone a doo-doo head and slamming the door might be to the point, but it isn't particularly nice.

One reason why we as fathers need to be very surefooted in this middle ground is because it is a place our children rarely go. For them, everything is felt in extremes: "I always have to . . . ," "I never get to . . . ," "I hate this . . . ," "I hate you . . . ." Our job is to supply the perspective. Sometimes, after listening to a string of emphatic definitives, it takes a great deal of discipline to refuse to get sucked in, and at the same time remember that this really is how he or she feels.

*One night at dinner, my daughter asked if she could
go on a three-day trip with a bunch of girls from her
school. It was over a weekend we had already committed to visiting my parents, so I said something like,
"I'm sorry, honey, but we already promised your
grandmother we'd spend the weekend at their house."
Bam! It was like the end of the world; she went
running from the table in tears and had a major
wailing fit for about an hour.*

Children are a roiling whirl of human potential, and it is all
in there. They have the capacity for extraordinary kindness
and jaw-dropping meanness. They can be the sweetest, most
tender little souls and the most ruthless, self-centered creeps
you ever imagined. In some fundamental way, they need to
try out all these variations to experience for themselves the
range of human possibilities. It is our job to provide some
guidance in that undertaking. That's why good fathering
means being able to consistently find and hold the middle
ground, and from there, extend ourselves to our children
with compassion and understanding.

That said, it is equally important to acknowledge that
ours is truly mission impossible—perfect parenting simply
cannot be done. It is not unlike playing a video game that is
hooked up to the world's most powerful computer, which is
programmed to win even if it has to change the rules
arbitrarily—you can't do it. You will make mistakes, you will
forget that they are the kids and you are the parent, you will
hurt their feelings, and you will lose your temper, your

patience, your understanding, your compassion, and your ability to cope. And sitting amid that messy pile, you will find every other father who ever lived sitting next to you.

I don't even remember what I was upset about, but what I do remember was yelling, "I'm going to knock your block off!" As soon as those words were out of my mouth, I was horrified. The worst part is that those weren't even my words—that was what my father used to threaten me with all the time. I knew how bad it had made me feel and here I was, repeating his threat to my own son.

This, too, is a gift. Recognizing that we are going to blow it makes it so much easier to do the real job, trying with all our heart to be the best father we can be. It also makes it so much easier for our children to accept their own mistakes, when they get front-row seats at Dad's big-screen screw-ups. Our wrong turns, harsh comments, general ineptitude, or plain bewilderment are simply another chapter of life's lessons, particularly if we can own up to our mistakes. Depending on how attuned we are to the effects of our behavior, the chapter may be titled "The Fine Art of Making Mistakes Gracefully" or, conversely, "Father's Folly."

My parents split up when I was four, and for the next three years, I didn't see or hear from my father. Then all of a sudden he was standing there in the driveway. Before I even knew what was happening, I had run over and jumped up into his arms. I was crying and he was crying and he just kept saying, "I'm sorry, I'm sorry, I'm so sorry."

That we will make mistakes is a given; but the relationship between a father and his children is one of nature's most resilient bonds. Calm down and all is forgotten. Apologize and we are forgiven. Return and we are welcomed. Extend our hands and we are embraced. The power, the permanence, and the forgiving quality of the love between our children and ourselves is nothing short of miraculous. Our job is simply to be as good a father as we can be, and that can be tough enough.

Unfortunately, many of us believe that we can be both a good father *and* consistently loved and appreciated by our children. It is a father's fairy tale. In our minds, we see ourselves patiently explaining to our twelve-year-old daughter why it really isn't such a good idea for her to go to that overnight "mixed" party, and she looks back at us with love and understanding and gives us a sweet, appreciative goodnight kiss as she trots off to bed.

Truly this is fantasy of the highest order. Our job is to use our best judgment to take a stand for our children, even in the face of highly dramatic and often painful protests from them. The rewards of fathering are not always immediate, but they run deeply through time. Ours is a lifetime enterprise, a labor of love that exists in the present moment as well as in the commitment to a future still decades away.

My son was a TV addict. Given his druthers, he'd turn on the damn tube the minute he got home and it wouldn't go off until he went to bed. We finally agreed that he could watch two hours a day and that was it. We set up a sign-in sheet, where he was supposed to record his hours. One day I came home—his mother was out—and I could hear the TV blaring as I came in. He instantly turned it off and pretended like it hadn't been on. I casually walked by and put my hand on the TV, and from the heat I could tell that it had been on for some time.

That night as I put him to bed, I told him he had lost his TV privileges for the week because he had watched more than his share that day. He not only denied it, but got all indignant when I didn't believe him. Every bone in my body wanted to just let it go, but I couldn't. I had to put up with him storming around the house for a whole week like a victim of the gravest injustice.

Finding the strength and willingness to hold onto that position is one of the most important responsibilities we assume as fathers, and it is often the most difficult. We must be willing to put ourselves, and our deepest feelings and beliefs, smack dab in the middle of our children's firing line: This is who I am, this is what I believe is right for my children, and this is important enough to me that I must insist on it. They will disagree, argue, and glare with anger and disbelief at how we could be so unfair. Harsh words may

be spoken and rash threats made; occasionally, particularly
if Mom is an unwitting participant in their manipulation,
their threats will be carried out.

*My daughter lived with her mother and stayed with
me every other weekend and for a couple of months
during the summer. By the time she turned eight, she
was almost completely out of control. Her mother
catered to her every whim and never disciplined her.
She would arrive at my house with this giant chip on
her shoulder. Then she'd sort of run through a set of
demands until she found one I wouldn't go along
with. I'd explain as clearly as I could why she couldn't
have only ice cream for dinner or stay up till midnight
or whatever the particulars were. Then she'd try to run
to the phone to call Mom. It was a real mess.*

*For a couple of years, most of our time together was
spent in a power struggle. Finally, she escalated to a
level that almost broke my heart. She made it clear
that she didn't want to visit me anymore if she
couldn't get her way. I had to tell her that because I
loved her so very much, I could not and would not do
anything as irresponsible as that. I wanted her to be
with me as much as possible, but when she was here
she would have to obey my rules.*

*It was a terrible time in my life because I missed
her so much. I'd call her, and sometimes she would
just walk away from the phone. She was very strong
willed as a child, and still is; and her experience with*

her mother was that if she held out long enough, she
would get her way. I think she just couldn't believe
that I wouldn't fold. It took her nearly a year to realize
that no matter what, I was going to be her father—even
if she never spoke to me again. One day when she was
eleven, she called and said she wanted to live with me.
That was eight years ago, and I've never had a serious
battle with her since.

These are the times when it is most painful to do our job
right, when the immediate result is that we are deprived of
the very thing that gives us the strength to be a good father
in the first place—a deep emotional connection with our
child. It is made all the more difficult because there is no
magic rule book of parenting we can turn to for answers.

There are, of course, plenty of "rules" associated with
parenting, most of which we try our best to impose, because
we believe they are healthy and necessary—bedtimes, limits
on television access and content, basic rules about meal-
times, chores, and so on. This, too, is an important part of
our job. If, however, the key to good parenting was simply
coming up with the best set of rules and enforcing them
consistently, it would be a very easy job indeed. As every
father who has ever pinned a diaper or done battle over "Big
Bird" burnout knows, the real art of parenting is practiced in
the cracks and crevices of these rules, for that is where our
children live.

One morning, I spent a full hour trying to thwart my

*daughter's burning desire to pull every single book out
of the bottom shelf of my bookcase. She'd crawl right
for it, then when I blocked her way, she'd make a
circuitous route through the kitchen. I'd haul her into
another room and try the old distraction trick, and as
soon as she thought I was distracted, she'd be out the
door and making a beeline for the bookshelf.*

One of the most natural instincts of growing children is
identifying and gravitating to the very edge of acceptable
behavior and then going beyond it. For children, rules exist
primarily as a way of defining the territory that will be
disputed. Try telling a toddler no and then watch closely.
Their eyes get big, partly in disbelief at your audacity and
partly in sheer joy at the challenge posed. Indeed, this
phenomenon of testing boundaries is the defining force in
our relationship with our children. We may like to think of
ourselves as in control, calling the shots and wisely laying
down a safe and healthy pathway, but in truth we will spend
most of our active fathering time rocked back on our heels
and gasping for breath.

Our children enter this world unable to do anything—
and they spend the next twenty years trying to make up for
it. They are single-mindedly dedicated to stretching boundaries. Like little fighter pilots testing the capacity of their
equipment, they need only know where the barriers are in
order to try shattering them. This headlong dash through life
forces us into the crucial but uncomfortable position of
being the resistance to their force.

Becoming comfortable with providing consistent discipline is one of the most difficult aspects of fathering. The job description sucks, the hours are long, you're always on call, and it is irritating to be constantly put in the position of having to say no. It is also one of the most important roles we will ever play. Our children are like speedboats with defective rudders. They have tremendous stores of energy, and the throttle is jammed at full speed ahead. The only thing that keeps them from roaring up onto the rocks is our firm and consistent guidance.

My son was three when his mother and I broke up. I felt so guilty that when he was with me, I spoiled him rotten. His reaction was to get more and more out of control. The sweetest little boy in the universe was turning into a complete monster right in front of my eyes. One day, a good friend who had witnessed some of this behavior told me to stop feeling so damned sorry for myself and start being a father again.

It was like having a bucket of ice water poured on my head—this poor kid was in a complete panic because I wasn't doing my job of establishing limits. By then, he was so unsure of me that it took three days of escalating warfare before he was finally convinced that his father had returned. Once he realized that I wasn't going to allow him to get away with anything anymore, it was like night and day—he went from acting like the possessed child in the Exorcist back to his old sweet self.

Our role as disciplinarian is to make our children's world safe enough so that they can spread their wings and fly. We protect them by establishing limits, by not allowing them to expose themselves to dangers we know they are not ready for. At the same time, because we are there, establishing and enforcing the necessary limits, they know that they are free to take risks. If we do this balancing act well, we will always keep our children's expanding world large enough to be challenging, but not so vast that they become lost.

For many of us, discipline triggers very different images: the hard-nosed, fear-inspiring, no-nonsense drill sergeant kind, or an idealized image of a wise and dispassionate sage, listening thoughtfully and resolving all conflicts with calm artistry. One works well in the army, and the other works on TV, but neither has much to do with the realities of raising children.

My memories are overflowing with days and weeks of punishment I endured after being summarily tried and sentenced by my father. The last thing in the world I wanted to be to my kids was the hard guy. Yet it seems like every time any real discipline was called for, my wife would hand it to me and walk out of the room. First I tried reason, only to discover that toddlers don't reason the way I do. Then I realized that sometimes being the ogre is an inescapable part of being the father. It's still tough to figure out where to draw the line, but at least I have accepted it as part of my job.

At the heart of good discipline is passionate teaching, and the most passionate teaching can take place when the need for discipline arises. Passionate because these are our children, and we must do our very best to prepare them for life. Passionate because they are our children, and it is in them that we can create our most meaningful legacy. Passionate simply because they are our children.

It is when the need for discipline arises that we can teach our children how to make their own decisions. It is when we can pass on our own heartfelt lessons and values and our beliefs about how life should be lived. It is at this highly charged moment that we can show our children the validity of their feelings, and show by example that even when emotions are high and seemingly very much at odds, they can and should be shared.

One night toward the end of my son's senior year in high school, I was on the telephone, trying to track him down after he failed to check in at the appointed time. I ended up talking to the mother of one of his friends and I made some comment about grounding him as soon as I could find him. She asked me where he was going to college and when he was leaving. We ended up talking for about an hour—two slightly panicked single parents—and by the end of the conversation, I realized that it was pretty damn late in the game for me to be thinking about punishment.

He was about to go off to college, and I had already pretty much done what I could to teach him my values and prepare him for making his own decisions. It's funny, there was a part of me that didn't want to give that up, because in a way it meant giving up my baby to the world. A few minutes after I hung up, the phone rang and it was my son. He apologized for being late checking in; he was helping a friend fix his car and lost track of the time. Then he told me he had been trying to get through for the last hour but the line was busy. Then he wanted to know if there was anything wrong. I told him everything was just right, including his father's separation anxiety.

Through our passionate teaching, by being as clear as we possibly can about actions and consequences, and then being as consistent as we can about enforcing those consequences, we can encourage in our children a strong moral foundation. Through our passionate teaching, by respecting our children's feelings and helping them articulate them, even when what they are feeling is anger at us for some real or imagined offense, we can encourage our children to be fearless about what they feel.

One very well-kept secret about discipline is that far from being the most dreaded aspect of parenting, it can be its greatest gift. There are few other places in your life where you will be so completely, totally, and passionately engaged. Of course, in practice, striking the proper balance can be incredibly difficult. There is a fine line (which our teenaged would-be attorneys will argue over for hours) between an appropriate restriction and an arbitrary rule. To complicate things further, what one day is a perfectly appropriate restriction can suddenly become a counterproductive arbitrary rule. For example, it may make perfect sense to require a small child to come directly home after school, but at some point in their educational career, that rule will become more an indicator of our lack of trust than a sensible precaution. It takes extraordinary ability to keep current with our children's headlong rush toward adulthood.

Sometimes my daughter would blow up over absolutely nothing, find grave injustice in anything I said or did, burst into tears, or retreat into sullen withdrawal—all for no reason I could decipher. When that happened, I felt like I had to be Sherlock Holmes, taking this discordant clue (courtesy of her outburst) and knowing that something was bothering her. I figured that my job was not to react to the display of emotion, but to the fact of it. Then I'd circle around as gently as I could and probe until I discovered that the class turtle had died today, or that she was angry at me because I couldn't make it to her soccer game three weeks ago, or that her best friend wasn't her best friend anymore.

Like most things of quality, this process gets increasingly complex over time. As our children grow, their emotional state becomes more complicated and their limits must change accordingly. We need the skilled timing of an orchestra conductor. Today's appropriate limits become tomorrow's unfair and overly restrictive rules; what's worse (or perhaps better), is that our children can tell the difference, even though they seem to protest the reasonable limits just as loudly as the unreasonable ones. After all, underneath this ritualistic struggle over boundaries is a cooperative effort: they want reasonable limits so they will feel like someone is looking out for them, and we want them to be able make wise choices and walk through life's mine fields unharmed. We are both trying to get to the same destination, only their job is to push forward with all the energy they can, whereas ours is to try to prevent them from outstripping their actual capacities.

Our children instinctively know this, which is why—despite their best arguments and an occasional flat-out tantrum—they accept our limitations with relative grace. The danger of imposing one too many unreasonable limits is that we will lose that acceptance. If our children come to believe that we really are unreasonable, that we are holding them back and not letting them spread their wings, they feel that they *must* stop obeying if they are to grow and develop. However, they still aren't ready to do it on their own. The result is a dangerous breach of trust. If out of fear or ignorance we are being overly restrictive, they will know it, and therefore ignore *all* our limits—and end up exposed to dangers they truly aren't prepared for. The worst part is that this is *our* mistake, not theirs. It is our responsibility to maintain their faith in our good judgment.

My dad wouldn't let me go anywhere or do anything. He had grown up in the country and was convinced that the city was a dangerous, evil place. It wasn't a matter for discussion or negotiation, it was just no. Finally, I gave up asking and just snuck out. The last two years I lived at home, I was out almost every night, and he never knew. The truth is I'm lucky I didn't end up in big-time trouble, because I was really out there on my own without too much in the way of sense to keep me in line.

One final level of complexity is the addition of more than one child. The younger one doesn't understand why the limits are so much more restrictive for him than for his older sister. Alternatively, the younger sister is different in some ways from her older brother, and now he resents her being able to do at age six what he couldn't do until age seven. No matter how well you figure out the fine balance of each child's expanding universe, you will be subject to what can feel like nonstop carping, complaining, and whining.

In fact, the whole process felt very much like trying to juggle ten flaming stakes while walking the high wire, with all the circus clowns tossing water balloons at you all the while. I knew I was going to get wet, I knew I was going to singe my fancy father costume, and I knew I would undoubtedly land on my head in the safety net now and then.

Fathering is not for the weak of heart. As our children grow and test their limits, they push us beyond ours. They delight us, scare us, amaze us, shake us to the core, and overwhelm us. Just to keep up with them, we need to be focused, flexible, on our toes, and in balance at all times, because you never know what is coming.

The only thing we are certain of is that to do it right, we have to put everything on the line. Traditionally, one of father's roles is to teach the importance of taking risks. The very best way to teach that lesson is to risk everything—our ego, our heart, our dignity, our pride—anything and everything we value to be the best father we can be.

Chapter 6

The Thrill of Knowing Your Children Deeply

I don't know what I was expecting. I guess I thought babies were all pretty much the same and then they gradually grew into distinct personalities. But when the nurse handed my daughter to me in the delivery room, it sent chills down my spine. There she was, hot out of the womb, eyes wide open, staring right at me; and it was so obvious that inside this tiny bundle was a very distinct and strong person.

Who is this miracle? How much of the individual personality of an infant is in the genes, how much is learned behavior, and, for lack of a more descriptive word, how much comes from the soul of this tiny child? These are a fascinating bundle of questions of which there seems to be endless debate among biologists, psychologists, social scientists, and theologians. From the viewpoint of parenthood, this is one of the great mysteries of life. For it is one thing to understand where babies come from, and quite another to understand where *this* baby came from.

We can all accept the notion that each of us is a distinctly unique individual, but sometimes it is difficult in practice to comfortably extend that acceptance all the way back to birth. This probably stems from our overemphasis of language: We are waiting for an explanation, whereas our preverbal children aren't waiting for anything. As adults, we feel seriously handicapped and emotionally deprived if we are unable to speak the language of infants and toddlers with any degree of skill. Some of us are lucky enough to get a crash course.

My wife had some fairly serious complications when our son was born, so she stayed in the hospital and he and I went home. For two weeks I was on round-the-clock duty. It was incredibly exhausting and probably the most amazing two weeks of my life. I always thought babies just slept, ate, and cried. I never had a clue how much other stuff was going on. Every day was an adventure for him; I felt like I could see him trying to get some control over his body, trying to figure out where noises were coming from and what they meant, trying to get all these visual images under control. It's really hard to put into words, but by the

time my wife got home from the hospital, I felt like I
really knew a lot about him. I could tell the hungry cry
from the tired cry from the wet-diaper cry from the "I
want attention" cry.

We also have a tendency to overestimate the effects of
genetics. This is a kind of ego-driven blindness that can be
particularly pernicious in parenting. From the obvious physical bequests of genetics—"he has my eyes" or "she has her
mother's nose"—it is a short, wobbly, and usually very
inaccurate step to "he's just like me" or "she's just like her
mother." Suddenly, your poor child is saddled with all your
habits, strengths, weaknesses, preferences, and peculiarities.
That's a very heavy load for a child who can't even speak up
to defend himself.

There we are, proudly projecting a very powerful image
of how we see our children, and the message they receive is
that this is what they are supposed to be, this is what will
make Dad happy and proud. Because making us happy is so
important to our children, they end up wasting an enormous
amount of time and effort, trying to cram themselves into
the mold we created instead of exploring and developing
who they truly are.

A few years back, one of my best friends died from
cancer. He had been really into athletics, and when
his son was born he started playing catch with him
almost before he could stand. It became the center of
their relationship. His son was always one of the best

baseball players around, and in his senior year of high school, he was offered a signing bonus to play for a major-league farm club. By then, the son was very angry with his father for all the reasons one can imagine and, partly to spite him, decided against signing the baseball contract. It created a huge breach between them.

A few months later, the son started thinking about what it would mean to his own life to have not even tried, and he changed his mind. Then he found out that there is an unwritten rule among baseball clubs that if someone is offered a contract, doesn't sign, and then changes his mind, it's too late, because they think it means he won't have the drive necessary to really excel. The boy ended up getting involved with drugs and was arrested a couple of times. He and his father hardly ever spoke, and at the end, his dad died very much alone and estranged.

This pit is very easy to unwittingly fall into, and the long-term results can be disastrous. This is one reason why it is so important for us as fathers to do our own emotional work. We must be very clear about who we are and what our needs are, and we must be certain that we do not unconsciously burden our children with our expectations. They are far too young and impressionable to sort out our expectations from their own, the things in life that interest and excite *them.*

Putting pressure on our children to be like us or, even worse, to be what *we* wanted to be but never quite succeeded at, can be doubly handicapping. It does not matter what the expectation is: to love to read, to be outgoing and charming, to enjoy fishing, to succeed in business. Anything that we impose as a vision for their lives will more than likely set them up to fail, set us up for disappointment, and confuse and derail their own development.

My father was a doctor, his father was a doctor, both my uncles are doctors, my older brother is a doctor . . . what choice did I have? I got halfway through medical school before I got up the courage to quit, and then it took almost ten years for me to get my bearings and figure out what I really wanted to do with my life.

Wanting our children—particularly our sons—to follow in our footsteps is an unconscious tendency that we fathers fall into with much greater regularity than mothers do. Perhaps it is the tangible proof we seek that something of who we are has been passed on. Mothers, on the other hand, need only remember the powerfully intimate day of their children's birth. It may also be our concern that they "do something meaningful" with their lives, which we all-too-easily translate into doing what *we* did. Whatever the reason, it is a potentially dangerous trap that should be consciously avoided.

Children are such energetic and eager learning machines that it is very easy for us to get dragged into believing that we are somehow in charge of directing their growth and development, somehow "molding" them. We aren't and we shouldn't be. Yes, we need to provide guidance, establish limits, and encourage their sampling of a wide range of interests, but it is *their* lives, *their* needs, and *their* interests that we need to become attuned to, not the other way around.

When my daughter was seven, her room suddenly sprouted Cubs paraphernalia like a fungus. She traded some of her things for a huge poster of Ryne Sandberg, a friend gave her his extra Cubs baseball cards, and she was dutifully clipping articles and pictures out of the newspaper. On her birthday, I gave her a Cubs hat, and it became a permanent fixture on her head. What was strange is that neither I nor my wife were at all interested in baseball.

A guy I worked with had season tickets to the Cubs games and one day he offered me his tickets for a Saturday game. I came home that night and told my daughter that since she was such a big fan, we were going to a game, but she had to promise to fill me in on who was who since I wasn't really up on the team. I will never forget the glow on her face. She was absolutely thrilled to be going to a real Cubs game, but the real thrill for her was that this was hers—she was taking me to see something she was really into.

Ultimately, what our children need from us most of all is to be acknowledged and loved for who they are. This is a sacred undertaking. If we do it well, we will provide them with lasting comfort. We will send them into the world knowing they are not alone, with confidence and sense of self-worth that will allow them to live their lives fully and joyfully. If we do it poorly, we will send them out into the world lacking the confidence and self-esteem to identify and pursue that which is necessary and important to them.

> *When my kids were growing up, I guess I was pretty rigid about what they could and should do. That's how I was raised, and I thought that was how you should do it. My daughter ended up marrying this guy who tried to control her entire life—from the clothes she wore to what she did with her time. It was really hard to take, but I kept quiet because I didn't feel it was my place to say anything. She ended up getting a divorce after four years and about four thousand dollars worth of therapy. At one point, her therapist asked me to come in for a session, and after letting me go on, complaining about her ex-husband's behavior, she said, "Well, wasn't he just picking up where you left off?"*
>
> *It was like a blow to the head. I didn't want to believe it, but it was so damned obvious—right down to the specifics.*

One of our deepest human needs is to be truly known and truly loved. That's why dedicating ourselves to learning who our children are and loving them for their uniqueness is our

most basic duty to them. If we fail, the message, intended or
not, is that they are not worthy: If your own father could not
or would not take the time to really get to know you, then
surely there must be nothing of value to know.

It is a sacred duty, but it is also one of life's greatest
pleasures—children are like an endless Christmas present.
Beginning on the day of their birth and continuing throughout our life, we are privileged to be an intimate part of the
never-ending unfolding of a human being.

To do it right, we need to remember that we are a part of
a very complicated and intense learning process. Our children start by learning how to control their bodies—how to
grasp, how to crawl, how to walk. They quickly progress to
learning sophisticated human skills, from talking, abstract
thinking, and identifying and expressing emotions to the
intricate human dance of interaction. The more skilled they
get, the better able they are to understand and clearly
articulate who they are and what particular combination of
desires, passions, dreams, and needs makes them unique.

We are given the great honor of participating in this
blossoming, and if we do our part well, we can be an
invaluable resource in helping, encouraging, supporting,
and guiding them. But from our very adult perspective, we
must remember that at the heart of this adventure is their
learning, their discovering, their coming to full, vibrant
consciousness about who they are.

On this journey, we do not and cannot have the answers.
However, by watching our children with fascination as their
answers emerge, by eagerly questioning them about how

they feel, what they think, what interests them, we show them that their journey of discovery is tremendously important to us. Through our avid interest, we communicate to our children that truly, deeply knowing them is a source of great joy in our life.

> *One of the best "secrets" of parenting I know I was taught by my daughter. She was seven at the time and, out of the blue, she came up to me and said, "Ask me a question." So I asked, "Who's your boyfriend?" and she said, "Dad, I'm only seven." "Okay," I said, "Who's your best friend?" "Debbie," she replied. Right then and there I realized that I didn't know that fundamental thing about her. Here was my beautiful, sweet daughter whom I would die for, and I didn't even know her best friend's name! We spent the next two hours with me acting like a kid, asking a million questions for every answer she gave me. She was giggling away, and I learned more about my daughter in two hours than I had in years.*

Most of us are pretty good at asking probing questions of strangers at cocktail parties or business functions. We learn early on that when someone is interested enough in who you are to ask even somewhat revealing questions, most people, flattered by the interest, are more than willing to cooperate. Yet we rarely think to use this very simple and effective technique with our children. Maybe we get so burned out by their constant barrage of questions that we are afraid that

asking even one tiny, little question will trigger a new
avalanche. But that's just the kind of avalanche we need to
be truly connected.

*Here's my trick: The next time they start asking you
questions, start asking them questions right back.
Think of it as loving revenge. We may have a lot more
of the boring, practical answers they are after (how
come hot water comes out when you turn the red
handle and not the blue handle?), but they have a lot
more of the answers we are really interested in. What
do they want to be when they grow up? What makes
them happy? What is their most favorite thing? Their
most favorite place? If they could go anywhere in the
world, where would it be? If they could do anything,
what would it be? If they could be anyone, who would
they be? If they ran the world, what rules would they
have? What changes would they make? What makes
them sad? Angry? What's their favorite color/animal/
song/television show? And for every answer you get,
ask why.*

A word of caution: Don't assume that what you learn today
will be true tomorrow. These dynamos change self-images
like chameleons, shed hobbies faster than a snake sheds skin,
and change directions faster than a pinball: Today he hates
apples; tomorrow he'll swear he's always loved them and
what's wrong with you that you don't know that?

It's particularly important for us to let go of the blunders, mistakes, and embarrassments of our children's past (even if the past was just last week). Childhood is a time of frantic experimentation and (hopefully) daring yet reasonable risk taking. Kids will make mistakes and fall on their faces; they will say and do things that no one would ever want to be reminded of. It is our responsibility to remember . . . and to forget.

It takes a lot to keep current with this whirlwind of change, but it is well worth it. We get a guided tour of the world through very wide eyes while exercising our perhaps long-dormant flexibility. Best of all, each swerve successfully maneuvered, each switchback survived, bonds us closer to the hearts of our children.

One of the greatest untapped resources of fathering is our ability to tell stories. Storytelling is in our bones. From man's earliest days, huddled around campfires, it was through storytelling that we passed on information and taught the next generation. It is still one of the most powerful tools at our disposal, and one that our children love.

I fell into stories quite accidentally. I used to read to my kids every night, but this one time my son had come with me on a trip and we had forgotten to bring any of his books. He was, of course, insistent that he get his story, so I just made one up. I remember that the hero was a wild boy about his age, named Fritz. He loved it so much that when we got home, he kept

*asking me for more Fritz stories. By the time my kids
grew out of stories, I must have populated an entire
fantasy world with characters.*

In the telling of stories, we create new worlds that capture
our children's interest and invite their participation. Great
stories throughout history have been used to teach, but they
can be just as important a tool for building and reaffirming
connection. The new and exciting world of interactive CD-
ROM can't hold a candle to the interpersonal interactive
capability of storytelling. We can create a context, a situation, bring it to a point of decision, and then invite our
children to choose a path. With that, we have them invested
in the world of our story. Then we get to twist them around
in our fantasy world, asking them again to make choices,
take risks, and, most important, stretch their imagination
and have fun. And we are doing it *together*.

Fantasies, historical sagas, moral tales, wild and crazy
adventures, scary stories, mysteries, stories without endings,
stories without purpose—it is in the telling, the listening, the
imagining, the squealing, hugging, screaming, and laughing
that we weave deep and beautiful connections with our
children. And it is in those magical moments of sharing that
we get glimpses into the deepest parts of who they are.

*I loved being a father. I loved rolling around on the
floor with my kids when they were young. I guess I
never thought that much about what I was supposed
to be doing. When I was growing up, it was all one*

*way: Fathers went to work, paid the bills, and were in
charge. That was it. When my kids became teenagers,
suddenly it was like they were from another planet. It
seemed like the only times we ever talked was when we
were in a fight. That wasn't the way I wanted it to be.*

With small children, asking questions and telling stories can
be a simple and enthusiastic process. With older kids,
however, particularly if you haven't already trained them
into accepting Dad as an interested participant in their lives,
it often requires considerably greater persistence and tact.
Ask a teenager a direct question, and more often than not the
answer will be one of the following four: "Fine," "Okay,"
"Yes," or "No."

It helps to remember that this truly is a tough time for
our children. They are passing through many very confusing
doorways. They need to leave the helpless humiliation of
childhood behind and lay the groundwork for an adult
identity—and it isn't easy, particularly with Dad and Mom
hanging over their shoulder. Our teenagers' sudden interest
in privacy and their lack of subtlety should not be taken
personally, but it does require some adaptation. Because if
we don't, we can quickly find ourselves very much outside
their lives, right when we may be more needed than ever.

*I felt like I always had a close relationship to my son,
but when he hit his teens, it was like he lost the power
of speech. I'd try to talk to him and all I'd get back were
garbled sounds and rolling eyes. That went on for a*

couple of years, and I was getting frantic, so partly out of desperation—just to see if I could get a couple of coherent sentences out of him—I told him I was thinking about buying some new stereo equipment to replace what he called my "antique" system. I couldn't shut him up. He got all excited and started telling me all this stuff about watts and hertz and crossovers—I had no clue what he was talking about, but God it felt great.

Although it is important to respect their need for more autonomy, it is critical that they know we are every bit as interested in their lives and committed to knowing, understanding, and supporting them as we have ever been. The process of inquiry simply needs to become more sophisticated, the communication methods more mature. Ask better questions, those that can't be answered with one word. Be willing to ask now and be answered later. Ask more questions about what *they* think and believe and feel, and respect their answers, even if you don't agree.

One of the most effective ways to get our children—particularly teenagers—to reveal themselves to us is to reveal ourselves to them. Tell them stories about your life—about things you worried about, mistakes you made, about being confused, being scared, taking risks. Tell them funny stories and sad stories, incidents that came out all right and those that were a disaster. The message is that they are important enough to know these intimate details of your life, that even their father had to go through these things, that you survived difficulties as a child, and they will too. When we are courageous enough to reveal to our children the unwashed stories about ourselves, it gives them the comfort of knowing that they can reveal themselves to us without fear.

> *When my kids were small, I told them about the time I sat imprisoned in my playpen, watching my mother spend hours meticulously transplanting all these flowers into her garden. Later that day, unobserved by my mother's usually very watchful eye, I managed to dig up most of her newly planted flowers in my enthusiastic attempt to play gardener. My youngest—who not coincidentally was usually the first one to get into trouble—loved that story and would beg me all the time to "tell the story about how you wrecked Grandma's garden."*

We know how much work fathering can be, but sometime we get so focused on it as *work* that we forget how much fun it can be. In fact, in emphasizing the work of fatherhood, something quite unintended seems to have happened. Being male in the late twentieth century means that, like it or not, we are judged most often by what we do. Our social identity comes not from what we hold in our hearts to be most precious and important, but from the work we do. Yet for more and more of us, what is most important is our role as a father. So the way we unconsciously choose to integrate these two worlds is by emphasizing the hardworking side of being a father: fathering is hard work, therefore, being seen as a father has value. But we can get caught up in our own charade and forget what extraordinary pleasure we get from this particular job. We start to believe our own posturing.

Then the weekend comes along and, tired of working, we end up ignoring our children in search of recreation for ourselves, forgetting that they are the ultimate interactive entertainment wonder. They are the very definition of *becoming*. It's like getting to watch a great work of art being created. Every day is an adventure of discovery, growth, learning, mastering, struggling, stumbling, groping, and backsliding. Before they even understand the questions, they are madly seeking answers, trying on different attitudes and characteristics, and exhibiting unbelievably focused attention that can last for seconds or persist for years.

When my son was three, he was completely fixated on this book called Bartholomew's Ten Thousand Hats. *That's all he ever wanted me to read. It was driving me nuts. I loved reading to him, but I started to dread bedtime, because I knew I was going to have to read that damn story again. Reading his bedtime story had become work, and that irritated me even more. Then I began to really pay attention to him while we went through the story. That was fascinating. I'd ask him to pick a book, and he'd very seriously retrieve* Bartholomew's Ten Thousand Hats. *Sometimes I hid the book somewhat, and he would tear the bookshelf apart until he found it. Then he'd sit down on my lap with it and get really focused. I began to notice*

*that there were some parts of the story where he'd get
very impatient and other parts he loved so much he'd
have me reread the page. I started asking him questions about which hats he liked, and found out that
he had very definite preferences for specific reasons.
The dreaded bedtime story turned into a fascinating
time for me. I think he stuck with that book for about
three months straight. It's not like I ever had any
brilliant insight into what he was getting out of it, but
it fascinated me to be able to see him involved in what
for him was a very focused and complicated proce-
dure.*

Once we get ourselves into the "fathering as work" mode, it's
hard to shake. It's too easy to let our interactions with our
children become obligatory instead of enchanting—a chance
to participate in the wide-open, rollicking adventures of
discovery that they truly are for our children. If we are
willing to dive into the experience of growing up with our
children, they can remind us how meaningful even the
simplest things can be.

*My daughter was at that age when kids just begin to
catch on that when a toy is out of sight that doesn't
mean it no longer exists. She had dragged a cookie
cutter out of a drawer and was playing with it. I
thought she might hurt herself, so I took it away. She
looked at me like I was one of the original robber
barons, and then got this look in her eye like the light*

bulb going on. She suddenly knew that the cookie cutter was around somewhere but had no idea where. We must have played with that cookie cutter for a hour straight. I'd hide it in my lap or pull it around the back of a chair, and she'd search for it until she found it. Sometimes she'd watch it disappear and then go looking at the place she had found it last time, instead of just following it into its hiding place, but pretty soon she had it all figured out. It was just incredible watching her; I could almost see the little gears whirling around in her head.

As a friend of mine once said, "Kids are a flat-out gas." As fathers we need to hold onto that truth with great consistency. Truly, deeply, enthusiastically enjoying our children is one of the fundamental building blocks of an enriching lifelong connection. Often, all we need do to really enjoy our children is remember that this opportunity to be with, and interact with them is not work but rather what we work *for*. When we approach each interaction with our children as a close encounter of the most fascinating kind, we are rarely disappointed.

This is as true for infants and toddlers as it is for ten year olds and teenagers. The process of growing up is an odyssey of truly epic proportions. In many ways, each child's development is a re-creation of our entire evolutionary path, from the physical phases of the fetus—complete with tail and fins— through the most basic struggles with language, right on into the more complicated lessons of social interaction.

That our children so desperately want us to play a starring role in their unfolding saga is a priceless opportunity that allows us to experience:

♦ The indescribable feeling of your infant's body when she relaxes completely onto your chest, snuggling her head into the crook of your neck.

♦ The thought that comes to mind as you're tying the final shoelace on that tiny foot while watching your toddler, trying to sit patiently, wrapped in sweater, coat, mittens, and hat, that this is probably the only time in his life that his clothing will weigh more than he does.

♦ The raw vulnerability exposed by your three year old when he solemnly assures you that if he really wanted to he could lift up the house.

♦ The combination of fear and disbelief that stops you in your tracks as you watch your five year old scampering up a tree with the agility of a monkey.

Enjoying your children can be like that compelling novel that you can't put down and can't wait to get back to. Their days are filled with wonder and excitement, and all we need to do to become captivated by the unfolding drama of their lives is allow ourselves to be drawn into their world as much as we can. Get involved in their studies, pay attention to what they are learning, to what bores them and what excites them. Allow yourself to be fascinated by the choices they make and to wonder what is around the next bend.

Sometimes little things crop up that take the fun out of our interactions with our children—their not enjoying an activity we do, arguments over money, fussiness, whatever. When that happens, we need to change the dynamics—and as soon as possible. Usually, there is a simple and obvious solution if we don't get caught up in the conflict. Change your schedule, change the activity, do whatever you can to change whatever has become the obstacle to sheer enjoyment: Stop playing one-on-one if your daughter is tired of losing (or let her win); stop swimming at the Y every day for exercise when your kids hate the water; take some outings close to home (or stay home!) if car trips always result in stress. Some things can't be changed, and giving up for the sake of our children all the things we enjoy is no solution either. But for every stuck situation we find ourselves in, there are invariably numerous alternatives that can be employed to the enjoyment of everyone.

For about a year, my time with my daughter was very strained and painful. What made it even worse was that she was living with her mother, so my time was already too limited. Her mother complained all the time about money, and that was obviously affecting my daughter, because every time we were together or talked on the phone, she asked me to buy something for her. I'm sure it was probably a kind of twisted way of trying to feel my love, and that upset me, because I didn't want her equating money with love. It also upset me because the whole process was beginning to make me feel like nothing but a checkbook. Mostly, it upset me because it was destroying our time together.

We finally solved the problem when I told her I would give her a lump sum for expenses every six months and that was it. She could use it however she wanted to, but I wasn't going to buy her anything other than paying for school expenses. Overnight, our relationship became a real pleasure again.

As fathers, we are doing great if we manage to stay on our feet while we madly maneuver to keep close to our kids. We can't afford to let obstacles slow us down, so we have to be sure that our time with our children is truly and mutually enjoyable. From that point, everything else will flow. One wonderful way to accomplish this is to let our children teach us all over again how to play.

My four-year-old boy always wanted to play "Chutes and Ladders" with me. I thought that was the dumbest, most boring game in the world. You'd spin the spinner, march your game piece up the squares, and then, completely by chance, either get to climb up a ladder or go sliding down a chute. Eventually, someone would get past all the chutes and win, but it always seemed to take forever. Then, as soon as one game was over, he wanted to play again. I couldn't understand what he got out of it. Actually, I realized that I wasn't getting anything out of it—I felt like I was wasting time. So then I started watching him, and the first thing I realized was here was a game that he was just as good at as anyone else. He knew the rules, could count out his moves, and won as often as he lost. It was finally being able to play on a level field that thrilled him. After that, it was easier for me to play along.

An odd thing happens when you grown up: You start being more concerned with results and less concerned with the process of arriving at them. There are many explanations for this, not the least of which is that in a world that elevates money to godlike significance, the result—the product, the sale, the price tag, the payoff—is all important.

In this arena, our children have much to teach us. For them, it is the journey that is most important—how something is done, the actual process, the interactions along the way—and arriving at the destination is just the icing on the cake.

One morning some years ago when I was visiting the ocean, I took a walk along the beach and saw a father and two small children with buckets and shovels, excavating a huge area for a sand castle. They all seemed to be having a great time, laughing and running around. Later that afternoon, I returned and saw the children wandering around picking up sea shells while their father was still hard at work, trying to complete the sand castle. By sunset, the kids and their mother had disappeared back into the beach house, and Dad was just putting the crowning touches on the castle.

In its own way, the above story is a poignant commentary on how easy it is to get fixated on results. I am sure, had he thought about it, this father would have said that spending time with his children was more important than finishing a sand castle that was going to be washed away with the night tide anyway. But he didn't think about it. He started building, and by god he wasn't going to stop until it was finished.

When we play with our children, we need to throw our expectations overboard and turn control over to the play experts—our kids. Playing need not be about teaching, about solving problems, or about building something. Watch any toddler: The best part about building a tower is knocking it down. Playing should be about enjoying ourselves, and it is an art form at which children are extraordinarily talented. Let them take the lead, but also be willing to invite them into your play.

I love baseball. Going to baseball games was something I did with my father and something I wanted to share with my children. It turned out that the one who got really hooked was my youngest daughter. By seven, she could keep score like a pro. She and I would go out to the park early for batting practice, and she'd chase foul balls in the stands; then she'd score the whole game. When we got home, she'd re-enact the key plays from her score card to her stepmother, who couldn't care less but loved hearing her imitate the radio announcer.

What is important when we invite our children into our areas of interest is to not demand or expect anything. Whether they comprehend the finer points of the game, understand the plot twist in our favorite flick, or truly appreciate the concert music is immaterial. The invitation is what's significant. It tells them that we love having them around, want them to know and be a part of our lives wherever possible, and that they're so important to us that we want to share our interests with them. But the last thing we want to imply is that they have failed us somehow by not loving the same things we love.

> When my son was ten, I took him on a trip to New York, just like I had taken his sister a couple years earlier. Our first day in the Big Apple was a disaster. I really wanted to let him decide what we would do, so we ended up walking all around the midtown shopping areas, then to the Upper West Side and Central Park; he wasn't having any fun at all. Actually, it was a miserable, drizzly gray day, and though usually I love to walk around New York, I wasn't having any fun either. By the end of the day, I finally realized that he was dragging us through a re-enactment of his sister's itinerary. He had heard her stories and was determined not to miss anything she had seen, but neither of us was enjoying it.
>
> The next day, I took over. At first he was upset, because he had us all set for a ferry ride. I told him that a ferry ride in a cold rain was not going to be great fun,

but I knew of a great art exhibit he would love. I will remember the look of horror on his face for the rest of my life. I think he was too shocked to even protest, but when we got there he wouldn't leave. It was an exhibit of "Mechanical Men"—incredible robots and wildly intricate constructions. He gave up on his sister's itinerary, and we ended up having a great trip.

Our children may share with each other a lot of DNA and environmental influences, but it is rare indeed to find siblings who are at all alike. It is almost as though the first thing a newborn does is check out any existing brothers or sisters and set about becoming as different from them as possible. Raising one child certainly gives us much of the skills and confidence we need to make fathering a second or third child a little easier; but in the most important areas— the ability to truly know and deeply connect with our children—it can be more of an obstacle than an aid: We get lazy, think we know more than we do, and make assumptions based on past experience.

Each of our children is extraordinarily unique. And though we may have that "I've done this before" swagger, we *haven't* done this before with *this* child—no matter *what* "this" is.

I've always been a very physical guy. With my first, I used to get into major rolling around on the floor— wrestling, tickling fests. We would laugh until we were exhausted. When my second child came along, I'd

*start roughhousing and she'd start crying. At first, it
really upset me. It felt like it was a rejection of that
part of me. Then one day, she crawled up into my lap
and snuggled in and gave me a huge smile. I thought:
Hey, this is not bad at all.*

Learning how to understand and communicate with different children is very much like learning different languages.
Some kids you can't shut up and others you can't get to talk.
Some are wound-up energy machines, while others are calm
and reflective. Some are highly sensitive to what is going on
around them, whereas others are completely oblivious to
everything but what they are doing. Some kids would watch
television from morning to night if you let them, while
others couldn't care less. They talk differently, move differently, feel differently, see the world differently.

*I've never been terribly athletic, never had much
interest in sports, and never understood people who
did. It was like an alien world full of strange behavior
and incomprehensible language. Then my daughter
came along. She was obsessed by sports from the word
go. When she was barely able to walk, she used to kick
this soccer ball that was about half her size around the
backyard for hours. For a few years, she played everything and anything—baseball, basketball, soccer, even
football. When she was ten, she finally settled on
volleyball, and that has been her passion ever since.
It would be very difficult for me to imagine some-*

one less like me than she is, but I am absolutely crazy about her. I always go to her games and listen to her explain all the strategy and complain about a teammate who isn't putting out the energy my daughter claims is necessary. It's just amazing. One day, I found myself screaming at the top of my lungs during a match, yelling at the referee for a bad call, and I thought, Oh! So this is what it's all about . . .

Our children give us so much, and one of their most surprising and welcome gifts is the open doors that were never open to us before. Through our children's differences, interests, and passions, we can enter foreign worlds and experience whole new ways of relating that are completely mysterious to us.

My father was a good man. He was well-meaning, proper, and reserved, but he had a very defined image of what his son should be, and I was not it. He wanted me to go into business or law or medicine, and here I was completely wrapped up in music. He was never angry or outspoken about it; he simply stopped talking to me, I guess because he felt like he didn't have anything to say.

When our children are like us in one way or another, it provides an avenue of connection that is simple and easy. When our children are not like us at all, however, it can be intimidating. We feel helpless in the father role that we are most comfortable with—that of teaching and guidance. What do we have to offer? We can't teach, because we don't know; we can't resolve the problems they come across, because the context is unfamiliar.

This can be a painful dilemma, but in truth it is an extraordinary opportunity. Often what our children need, what they ask of us, is to forget teaching and problem solving, leave the preconceived roles of fathering behind, and simply be with them in the moment, share this place that is their life. Let them know that even though you are different, their interests, dreams, trials, and heartbreaks are important to you.

The very fact that they are different from us is one of the great gifts of fathering. Together, with and through our children, we can open ourselves to discovery, to learning, to expanding our appreciation of those different from us; and we can do this without great emotional risk. They stretch our boundaries and contribute to our growth.

Chapter 7

Fathering with Respect & Honesty

You know what's strange? I hear so many stories from men about fathers who never told them they loved them. My father tells me he loves me, but ever since I decided not to follow him into medicine, he has never once spoken to me about what I do. To me, that is every bit as painful.

This fathering business is just not as simple as we all wish it were. Our gut tells us that if we truly love our children, everything else will sort itself out. Unfortunately, it doesn't always work out that way. Loving our children is undeniably the essential starting point, but we can't just sit back comfortably, knowing how much we love them, and expect everything to turn out all right. Our love for our children may be the fiber our relationship is woven from, but we still must show it. And it must shine through in bold, vibrant colors.

One important thread in that tapestry is what we live and teach about respect. For many men, the word itself is very charged. It is often used and misused in anger, but the concept plays a central role in a well-lived life.

I stepped off the stage at high-school graduation and six hours later was on the night shift on the factory floor. I worked my butt off to give my kids what I never had, and now my own college-educated son treats me like some bumpkin. I don't claim to be the most educated person in the world, but I'm proud of what I've accomplished and I don't need to apologize for anything I ever did in my life.

One reason it is so difficult to become completely comfortable with the concept of respect is that embedded within it are two distinct components that exist in a state of constant tension. For *respect* is a word both of connection and disconnection.

On the one hand, respect is the ultimate expression of our connection to one another in its most basic form—the regard we hold for all living things, simply because they are a part of the miracle of life. In that way, respect is given like the love we hold for our children, without conditions.

But respect also connotes distinctions between people, the fundamental measuring stick we use to separate those people we admire from those we don't. That kind of respect is conditional, based on the development of and adherence to a strong, individual moral code. From this place, we make judgments of others' behavior.

It is from the first, broader aspect of respect that most of our fathering must flow: We must respect the individuality of our children, their unlimited potential, and, always, their feelings. But it is the second kind of respect about which we must teach them, and through much more than just our words. It is our responsibility to teach our children the more complicated lessons of respect—about exercising moral judgment and making difficult choices—by our own example. As the old saying goes, actions speak louder than words.

From day one, my father and I were like oil and water. He was always in his head somewhere, and I spent the first eighteen years of my life mostly in my body. My senior year in high school, I was captain of the football team, and we were playing our biggest rival at the homecoming game. I begged and pleaded, and my father finally agreed to come to the game—a first. At the end of the half, we were tied at 14. On the first series of downs in the second half, I looked up from the field and saw my father leaving. At the end of the game, my mother tried to cover for him by saying he hadn't left until after the game was over, but I saw her sitting next to an empty seat the entire second half.

When we become a father, we are not asked to place an order

for the kind of child we want. They may be athletic or total klutzes, intellectual or academic underachievers, charming and outgoing or contemplative and shy, tall, short, gifted, or handicapped. Whatever unique combination we are given, they are our children; if we cannot respect them for who they are instead of who we may want them to be, it is our great failing, but our children will pay the price.

Respect is the acceptance and honoring of who the other person truly is. One way we can demonstrate that respect for our children is to remember the power of father, and to walk softly when we are in their world. At work, we are often rewarded for having firm and definitive opinions, but in their arena we need to remember that our opinions carry the weight of gods, and that can be very difficult for our children to gracefully bear. We may think their choice of TV programs or music or books is boring and uninteresting, but that does not give us the right to announce it or, worse still, denounce it.

My father lived five hundred miles away when I was growing up, but he had an incredible influence in my life. I must have gotten more mail than most of the adults on my block and I never had any idea what would show up next. I had subscriptions to the weird-est assortment of magazines. I'd get a catalog of electronics parts one day, a brochure on chinchilla breeding the next, and a copy of The Little Prince *in French after that. He wasn't much of a talker, but he'd call about once a week and ask what I thought about the tape of Balinese music or if I'd had a chance to fiddle with the calligraphy pen he sent.*

One of the time-honored roles of a father is to be the window to the world for our children. In fulfilling that role, we need to expose them to a broad range of interests and not restrict them by the boundaries we've chosen for ourselves. In that task, we are certainly aided by the rapid development of entertainment and communications media, but we are challenged at the same time. Our children are not growing up in the same world we came up in. For better and for worse, they are exposed to a much broader and, in some ways, a much harsher array of influences than we were at their age. We need to accept, appreciate, and work with the scope of that exposure and at the same time make sure that it does not become a substitute for our participation.

Bad television is an invitation to good discussion. News of war, natural disasters, or the ranting of posturing politicians is an opportunity for meaningful dialogue. Invite your children to participate in "serious" adult conversations whenever and in whatever manner seems appropriate. Ask their thoughts and opinions about the issues that arise, and treat their opinions with respect, even if you disagree. Respecting their opinions means it is all right to gently question why they hold a particular view, and you can certainly offer your own thoughts in as provisional a manner as possible, but it is not all right to say, "I completely disagree." Coming from Dad that is tantamount telling them they are stupid.

*One night we were watching television, and in the
coverage of a local election, there was a candidate
going on and on about cleaning up the streets and
getting rid of all these lazy homeless people. A few days
later, my twelve-year-old son and I were driving in the
car, and he made some comment about why this guy
we passed on the street didn't just get a job. I was really
stunned. The following week, I took him with me to do
an evening of volunteer work at a local food program
that serves hot meals to homeless people. It was a real
eye-opener for him to stand there and dish out mashed
potatoes to a long line of obviously very hungry people.*

Being a father requires a powerfully accurate sense of equi-
librium. We need to be able to constantly weigh options and
arrive at solid decisions with some consistency. One area
where it is easy to get out of balance is when it involves
"protecting" our children. Our role as protector is so fundamental that it is very easy to err by overprotecting our
children without even thinking. This can be very counterproductive. When we shield our children from some of the
harsher elements of the world we live in, we set them up for
shock and disillusionment. Once they are on their own, they
will inevitably encounter those aspects of our world, but
they will have to face them alone, instead of with the
reassuring comfort of Dad by their side.

It's important for us fathers to offer just the right amount
of protection—not too little and not too much. In that way,
we not only stretch our children's individual horizons and

broaden the context for their dreams, but we can introduce them to some critical skills for navigating around the shoals and riptides of life.

Over the years of parenting six kids, I've learned two things about what children should and should not be exposed to: First, our children are much more capable of understanding and processing information than we want to believe; and, second, they will grow up and leave much more quickly than we can possibly imagine. I decided that it made more sense to expose them to the world as it truly is but I make damned sure it's a guided tour. So as my kids go out into the world, I go with them—and there's plenty of conversation about what we see.

There are some things about our world that we need to show our children simply to let them know that they should ignore them completely. One area that looms large for fathers today is all the residual institutionalized gender bias that permeates our society. Between men and women this is often a heated and confusing issue. We have all spent long hours thinking and debating about everything from who should do what around the house to what the differences between men and women really are. Someday we might even approach some semblance of a consensus, but when it comes to our children, the issue is much more immediate. Any preconceived notions about what is or is not appropriate for girls as opposed to boys will, at the very least, seriously restrict our children's potential, and can be absolutely crippling.

> *The summer I was ten, my older brother played one particular jazz album almost every day. I don't remember who it was, but it had this haunting flute that would come in and out of the melody. I fell completely in love with the flute and pestered my parents for lessons. My father finally put an end to it by saying that the flute was for girls. After that, I never took any music lessons until last year when I started playing piano. I love it; it is so soothing and such an easy way for me to relax. I just wish I had started earlier.*

As fathers, we should open the widest possible window of opportunity for our children and not to allow the gender prejudices of the past to interfere. For many of us, that is not easy, because we ourselves have been subject to its effects.

> *When I was a child, I wore my feelings on my sleeve. That was quickly beaten out of me. I just turned forty and am only beginning to be able to know and express my own feelings again. I have a picture of my sister and me that I use to remind myself how I got here. It was taken on a Sunday visit to my grandparents' house when she was eight and I was six. It was just the two of us, me trying to hold back tears because my grandfather had just yelled at me, and my sister, a*

fierce tomboy, scowling in anger because my mother had made her put on a dress for the picture.

Now I find myself needing to avoid the gravitational pull of stereotyping my own children. When assigning household jobs, it's so easy for me to ask my daughter to clean up the dishes and my son to do the yard work. I have to keep remembering how much those stereotypes hurt me.

We need to consciously help and encourage our children to trample the boundaries. Teach your sons how to cook (or learn together), and your daughters how to throw a curve ball. Buy your daughter a tool kit and introduce your son to the mysteries of infant care that were denied to you. It doesn't matter if your son decides he hates to cook or your daughter can't throw a curve. The goal here is not to achieve some result; it is to go through the process of knocking down any and all barriers that might impede our children's happiness and development.

One of the oldest and most revered jobs of father is revealing the pathways to the future from which our children must someday choose. Being their window on the world is a traditional role of fathers, but the character of what that means has changed dramatically. The world is transforming and becoming more complex at an astonishing rate; and the one our children will inherit is vastly more intricate and holds greater danger—as well as possibilities—than even the world we grew up in just a few short decades ago. Respecting the unique potential of each of our children requires that we pay close attention to this part of our job.

> I used to hate the word feelings, *because every time I heard it, it meant I was going to be dragged into some long, brutal battle. A couple of weeks after my wife and I split up, I was sitting in my new, very empty apartment, thinking about my kids and tears just started rolling out of my eyes. It was absurdly funny— seven years of battles over my "repressed" feelings, and here I was, sitting all alone in an empty kitchen, bawling my eyes out.*

For fathers, for men, it is difficult to even begin a discussion about emotions without bags full of extraneous trash getting in the way. It is unquestionably true that most men, for whatever reason and by whatever process, are much more emotionally reserved than most women. In general, it is more difficult for us to clearly identify, freely articulate, and comfortably admit to the broad spectrum of human emotions. It is also true (or at least it *feels* true) that most of us have at one time or another suffered under the brunt of a very emotionally charged accusation that all the problems of Western civilization have been caused by our own personal difficulty expressing our feelings. To put it mildly, emotions have become a very charged issue for men and, as uncomfortable as it might be, one that we must address head-on.

In this often difficult undertaking of once again coming into full possession of our emotions, we are blessed with the best possible teachers—our children. Much of the time, children seem to run on little else *but* emotion. They cannot always accurately identify what they are feeling, but that is largely because they are so wrapped up in the feeling itself and they lack the vocabulary to articulate it. Helping our children identify, discuss, and respect their own feelings allows us to re-learn the same lessons we might have misplaced somewhere along the journey.

> *When I was ten, I was invited on a week-long camping trip by a friend. I wanted to go so badly, but my father wouldn't let me. It triggered the biggest fight we had ever had. I was really upset and kept arguing; he couldn't believe I was arguing with him and started to get more and more angry and abrupt with me. Then as it began to sink in that he was not going to let me go, I became furious, which really got him going. He absolutely couldn't deal with my feelings and kept saying that I was being disrespectful. I think I spent most of the next year restricted to my room.*

Because men have difficulty in the realm of the emotions, we often believe that our children are somehow being disrespectful to us when expressing their feelings. But feelings are neither right nor wrong, good nor bad; they simply are. They also constitute the most vitally important source of information about who we are and what we want.

> *I swear, teenagers are designed to be disrespectful. I remember once getting into a test of wills with my son*

*over the color of the sky that day. We were actually
yelling at each other about whether the sky was
whitish blue or bluish white! At times like that, it
helps to take a few deep breaths and remember that
this is about as difficult a time of life as there is. Here
he is, fourteen years old, stumbling on the doorstep of
adulthood with but the bare essentials in terms of
experience and resources to rely upon. Of course, he
wanted to think he's right about something.*

In truth, if we can manage a few more deep breaths and get
an even wider perspective, the teenage years are a most
extraordinary time to witness and to experience. As teens,
our children are like fledgling birds, tottering on the side of
the nest—not at all convinced that their wings will support
them but absolutely compelled to dive out into the void
anyway. All indications to the contrary, it is a time in their
lives when our supportive and persistent presence and can
make the difference between a bumpy but successful flight
and a painfully humiliating crash.

This is also a difficult time for many of us, because our
relationship to our children is undergoing dramatic and
permanent change. They are leaving us, and, whether we
want to admit it or not, that can trigger a turmoil of emotions
to rival any teenage outburst. We are afraid we have somehow failed to prepare them. We are terrified they will
stumble into disaster. We've grown to love the consistent,
warm glow of being their father and we are afraid it will go
away; or we haven't had enough opportunities to be with

them and we feel guilty. We watch their expanding orbit and are saddened by the realization that we are becoming less and less a part of their lives.

These are tough issues to deal with, and it is very tempting to dig in our heels in a vain attempt to slow the process down. But resistance is counterproductive—they are not going to be held back. Dad's attempts to reassert levels of control or authority appropriate to much younger children will only open a wider and more confrontational breach.

One day, my thirteen-year-old daughter came home with purple hair and an earring in her nose. I was furious. I stormed around, trying to figure out the proper response; among other options, I considered mayhem, shaving her head, and moving to Alaska. After I calmed down a bit, I realized that her hair would grow out and that it was unlikely she would keep it purple forever; and, while it was possible, I had a hard time imagining her as a grandmother with an earring in her nose.

The teenage years are the time for experimentation. Partly because it is so difficult and so important for teens to establish separation from us—so long their lords and masters and the center of their emotional universe—the urge to outrageous self-expression is almost too much to resist. Long hair, short hair, purple hair, no hair, tattered clothes, mismatched clothes, or baggy clothes—through music, fads, and friends, they are on a mission to explore uncharted territory and to appear as unlike us as they possibly can. It is our job to be sufficiently "shocked" to satisfy their need to shock us; grudgingly accepting to demonstrate our respect for their right to be whatever they want to be; and secretly overjoyed that they aren't getting themselves into any real trouble.

Of course, there are no guarantees that they aren't getting into real trouble, but we can greatly improve the odds by doing our part from the very beginning. It might be an overgeneralization to state that behind every seriously troubled teenager is a father who didn't do his job, but it wouldn't be far off.

Our children are like extraordinarily powerful rockets, and we are Mission Control. If we fail them when they are young—if we are unable to make solid and lasting emotional connections, if we do not teach them the scope and responsibility of their potential, and if we are unable to bequeath them a powerful sense of self-worth and self-respect—it is during their countdown to adult life that they will be in the most danger.

I was in high school, and things between my father and me were beginning to fray. One evening, he came into my room and said, "I want to talk to you about the hours you have been keeping." I was instantly defensive and irritated, because of course I was trying to head out the door to spend some of those late hours. Without missing a beat, he said, "Fine, give me time

within the next week when you can meet with me." It
was the first time my father had ever made an ap-
pointment with me. It made me realize that this
wasn't just a tug-of-war between us—I really had to
consider what he was saying.

At this juncture in their lives, we need to increasingly treat
our teenaged children as though they already are the responsible adults we want and expect them to be. We can't hold
on tight with both hands and then just let go and wish for the
best. Rather, we need to become more adept at granting
them more freedom and respecting their right (within reason) to control their own lives.

Here's what I've learned from dealing with my three
teenagers: deal with disagreements and conflicts
through negotiations rather than by issuing edicts
that probably won't be obeyed and certainly will be
resented. Give them plenty of real power in both the
procedures and the substance of those negotiations,
and they will be less likely to get completely out of
control.

Transitions are always tough. When our children were very
young, we made all the rules and enforced them because it
was necessary and because they needed to know that we were
there, setting boundaries and limits. Eventually, the time
comes for that authority to be handed over. It is no longer
necessary nor appropriate for us to make their rules, no

longer our job to impose our boundaries and our limits. We can no longer protect them from themselves. Our (hopefully fully prepared) children must begin assuming command and control over their own destinies.

> *About three days after getting my driver's license, I borrowed my father's car, went around a corner too fast, and wrecked it. I remember sitting in my room, absolutely certain that while I may have survived a collision with a tree, I was not going to survive facing my father when he got home. He kept me waiting for almost an hour after he arrived; when I think about it now, he was probably trying to calm down, because when he came into my room, he was completely calm. He looked at me with this kind of scared/sad look and just talked to me about growing up and being responsible. I was all ready to make excuses, and instead, the truth of everything he said just hit me right between the eyes.*

In the process of making this awkward and poignant transition with our children, we are forced to grapple with the second kind of respect, the conditional respect we hold for those we believe live their lives honestly, responsibly, and with integrity. We will always love and respect our children because they are our children. As they assume more and more control over their lives, they learn that as an adult, respect is conditional, that it must be earned.

Ironically, one of the notions about fathering that has

gotten badly twisted as it was handed down through the generations is that we deserve respect *because* we are fathers. Nothing could be further from the truth. We deserve respect as fathers only if we earn it—by demonstrating that we are good fathers. We are the adults and we are responsible and accountable for our actions.

My father used to yell at me, call me an irresponsible bum, and then sit in front of the television every night, getting drunk and yelling at my mother. As soon as I could, I left home and never looked back.

We can't expect to teach our children lessons we refuse to live by. "Do as I say and not as I do" won't cut it. We can't smoke, overeat, drink too much, ignore our health, and work too much and under too-stressful conditions and then expect our children to refrain from self-destructive behavior. They may choose different drugs or behaviors, but we will have been the model, and any objection on our part will be seen by them as the height of hypocrisy.

At the heart of this issue is the fundamental importance of always being honest with our children. Depending on the issue being discussed and the age of the children, that might involve a more-or-less complete answer. It might even involve a straightforward but honest refusal to discuss issues that you believe for one reason or another are not appropriate (like details of your sex life). What's important is that they know that what you do say to them can be trusted.

The importance of establishing that trusting bond of

honesty cannot be underestimated. Without it, our children are set adrift without moorings. If you can't trust your own parents, who in the world *can* you trust? Being scrupulously honest with our children lets them know that we trust them with the truth. It also inoculates them against one of life's most vicious scourges: people who bend or twist the truth in order to manipulate others.

> *My daughter is not the most athletic kid in the world, but she loves sports and works very hard at it. One day after one of her soccer matches, I was trying to be supportive and I got a little carried away, telling her how great she had played. Throughout my enthusiastic speech, she had her head down; when I finally stopped, she just looked me right in the eye and said, "Dad, I sucked and you know it." It caught me completely by surprise; I started laughing, and then she was laughing, and then she gave me a great, big hug and said, "Dad, I may not be much of a soccer player but I do always try my hardest."*

Our children are very good at knowing when we are telling the truth. Remember, we have been godlike creatures with seemingly awesome powers for most of their lives, and they have put some of that time to use, studying our moves and trying to understand and anticipate our thoughts and actions. We forget that as well as we know our children, in many respects they know us even better. They may not have an adult understanding of who we are, but they are meticulous students of what we do.

It is our actions more than our words that set into stone the patterns that most dramatically influence our children's lives. If we break our promises, even about what might seem to us to be small things, such as showing up at baseball practice or a school play, we are showing them that they are not very important and that broken promises are an acceptable part of life.

I never intentionally lied to my children but, looking back, I sometimes walked such a fine line—because of what I wanted to do rather than what I had to do— that only a lawyer could tell the difference. One day, I was on the phone to my son from work and I promised him I'd do everything I could to get to his game. He just scoffed and said, "Yeah, just like you always do." I never lied to him, but I sure as hell misled him and disappointed him.

Nowhere is this more true than in our relationship to their mother. If we are still living with their mother, we are modeling how a man and woman should be together. The nature and quality of that relationship will be the model that our children gravitate toward when they are ready to marry. We can't engage in constant verbal battles with our wife without expecting our children to think that this is what marriage will be like. We cannot treat our wife disrespectfully without expecting our sons to model our behavior in their marriages and our daughters to expect it from their husbands. We cannot silently suffer an unhappy marriage without expecting to pass on our legacy of misery to our children.

If we are separated or divorced from their mother, the way we interact with her will be the microscope under which what we say about honesty and respect is held up to inspection. What you cannot control does not matter—whether the divorce was amiable or contentious, whether your ex-wife is the most cooperative soul or the most vindictive, mean-spirited person in the world. What we *can* control, and therefore the only thing that truly matters, is how we act and what we say.

> My parents split up when I was very young. I lived with my mother for many years, and she never had a good thing to say about my dad. Yet every weekend he was there to pick me up, and he never said an unkind word about my mother. The worst thing he ever said was, "Your mother and I disagree about just about everything, but we both love you very much." When I was nine, I moved in with my father, and my mother couldn't understand why.

Our children possess a remarkable trait—they are able to recognize and gravitate toward that which resonates as most sincere and true. If we act respectfully and responsibly, if we behave toward our ex-wife with dignity, integrity, and compassion, ultimately that will be the lesson our children incorporate into their lives. Sometimes it is difficult, particularly if our ex-wife is actively trying to undermine or obstruct our relationship with our children. Sometimes it feels hopeless, especially if the children get dragged into an ex-wife's divisive manipulations. But if we want to be a good father, it is not optional behavior. The legacy of respect we pass on to our children has more to do with who we are and how we act than what we say.

Chapter 8

The Paradox of Challenge
& Acceptance

When I was in high school, I was very shy, and my father was always pushing me to get involved in this or that. There wasn't a whole lot I was good at, but I ended up training for the 440 in track. I knew I wasn't fast enough to run the sprints, and I didn't think I had the stamina for longer distances. At my first track meet, I was so pumped up I took off like a bat out of hell and was leading everybody. Then my legs turned to Jell-O, everyone raced past me, and I stumbled over the finish line dead last.

I was so ashamed, I felt like I had let my dad down. After the meet he came up and hugged me, and I blurted out something about how sorry I was. He looked at me with this totally surprised expression and said, "Son, you have nothing to be sorry about. I'm really proud of you."

Good fathering is not simple. You can't just follow a script or set of rules, and much of what you must do seems to involve constant tension from opposite directions. One place where that tension can surface on a daily basis is in our role as teacher or coach. It is our job to encourage our children to take risks, to expand their world, to expose themselves to new experiences; yet at the same time, it is our sacred duty to support them simply for who they are. Though it's easy to err in either direction, men often find themselves more in the pushing-and-prodding dimension than women do. We often experienced this with our own fathers and struggle to avoid doing the same to our kids, particularly our sons.

Nothing I did could ever please my father. In Little League, I was the best hitter on the team, and all he seemed to talk about were my strikeouts. I'd bring home a report card with four A's and a B, and he'd give me the "I'm so disappointed in you" look. I hate being a lawyer, and the only reason I went to law school was to please him. I'm forty years old, divorced, my life is in shambles, and I just realized that one of the reasons I married my wife in the first place was because my dad thought she was so great.

In reality, there is less tension between support and challenge than it may feel at times, because this base of unconditional support is what makes it possible for us to effectively and lovingly challenge our children to take risks. If we remember and express our love, if we follow our heart, we will know what to do in a given circumstance, whether to push or hold back.

I had been planning this trip in my mind for months. After moving away from where my ex-wife lived, I was having a hard time adjusting to not seeing my kids at least every other day. This was the first time they would be with me for a weekend, and I wanted it to be special, so I took them to this park with a huge, ancient merry-go-round. My two-year-old daughter's eyes just lit up; she would have gladly spent the entire day riding in circles on top of those big prancing wooden horses. My five-year-old son was another matter altogether. He was scared to death to even go near it. I told him he'd love it, but he was not at all convinced that those wooden horses weren't going to break free any minute and stampede across the park, carrying unsuspecting little kids (including his sister) with them. Many thoughts went through my mind, particularly those old gender-role stereotypes: Was my son a sissy? Should I try to force him to do it? But then I realized it was more important that he not feel pressured. So she rode the merry-go-round, he clung to

*my leg for safety, and I realized that at that moment,
it was how things should be.*

Our children need to know that we love them simply
because they are our children. They can make mistakes, be
scared and cry, lose every spelling bee or race, strike out in
the bottom of the ninth with the winning runs on base,
disobey, think bad thoughts, or spill their milkshake all over
the backseat of the new car—and Dad will still love them.

That unmovable, unshakable, unconditional love must
be as solid as a mountain of granite and as reliable as the sun
rising every morning. With that foundation, our children
are free to attempt the daunting array of seemingly daredevil
feats that make up the daily challenge of growing up: free to
take risks, to explore their world and their interests, to dream
of running like the wind or soaring like the eagles; free to
daydream, to collect pebbles or bugs, to wonder what they
will do when they grow up; free to invent games and change
the rules, and to make up imaginary worlds and populate
them with imaginary friends; free to dream themselves into
lofty positions of power and respect; free to change dreams
as often as they change T-shirts.

If our love is conditional, our children will feel as though
their very lives are built on shifting sands. All of their energy
will be focused outward, on trying to solve the mystery of
what they must do to be loved by Dad. Instead of spending
their time exploring and experimenting with the raw mate-
rial of their own personality, they become obsessed with
studying our every move and mood shift, the better to

anticipate what they must do to please us.

If we fail them here, by not providing a solid foundation of unconditional love, they grow up so outwardly focused that they lose track of their own desires. They will forget their dreams or, worse still, forget *how* to dream. They will never discover who they are and what they need in order to be happy. They will lose or never find the unique trajectory of their lives, becoming instead like satellites, always captured in the gravitational pull of some other body.

The more I live, the more I realize that being a father is a miraculous gift and an awesome responsibility. I know that if I and other men do our job well, we become part of a community of men helping to transform the world. If we do our job poorly, we pass on festering wounds that our children must bear and hopefully heal. I know the suffering I felt at the hands of my father and really try not to pass on similar pain to my children.

In this most basic function, it is not enough that we love our children unconditionally—we must let them know it over and over again. One way we do that is to clearly separate their endeavors and achievements from their being. Encourage them and support them in the things they do, but love them for the beautiful little people they are. For many of us, trained as we were in the male world of achievement, this is more difficult than it seems. We are very comfortable commending effort or celebrating a job well done, but aren't always that practiced at just weaving a strong, soft web of love.

> *When I was small, my father used to take me on long walks every weekend back in the hills behind our house. When we got to this one little knoll that overlooked what seemed to me at the time to be the most beautiful meadow in the world, he would reach into his pack and spread out a blanket. We would sit there, watching the meadow and eating our snack, and then we'd both lie down, me with my head in the crook of his arm. Sometimes I'd fall asleep and when I woke, the sun would have jumped across the sky. I think about those times a lot. I can still remember so clearly the feel of my father's hand and the smell of pipe tobacco clinging to his shirt.*

Just spending time with our children without having to do anything tells them that they are important, that just being with them is a pleasure for us. They don't have to entertain us, they don't have to perform, they don't have to do anything but be themselves.

One way of reinforcing their certitude about that safety net of love is by becoming masters of empathy. It is a challenge that is surprisingly rewarding. True empathy goes beyond simply understanding how our children feel. It is the emotional discipline of taking yourself outside of time, putting yourself in the position that *they* now occupy, and then actually *experiencing* their feelings. It might be the simple but overwhelming frustration of your youngest child, who's always at the bottom of the pecking order. It might be the feeling of confused rejection after an argument with a best friend. It might be the feeling of being unfairly punished.

The range of our children's emotions is quite broad, but the span of our own emotional experiences is considerably broader. We have been there and beyond. We have had the same or similar experiences. It is not difficult to call upon our memories in order to place ourselves in the proximity of their current position, and the benefits are extraordinary and immediate. When we experience their feelings, they cannot help but know it. And the better we get at sensing, decoding, and understanding the flow and texture of their emotions, the more they will feel known, loved, safe, and secure.

> *When I think about relating to my kid's feelings, I realize that it's like adjusting the horizontal hold on a television—first there is only a jumble of static, and suddenly the picture jumps into clear focus. If I get afraid, I won't be able to figure it out; but if I just relax into it, I'm usually able to do it. Sometimes it helps to go away from her for a while, a half hour or so, in order to be able to put myself in her position. Then I come back and have the conversation.*

When we are able to put ourselves in their place and feel what they are feeling, the rest is easy. Our children feel

deeply understood and received. Our willingness to feel—
rather than just understand—their feelings is both a demon-
stration of their importance to us and the proof of our love
for them. Why but for unfathomable love would anyone
want to reexperience the irrational anger, quivering fears,
mind-numbing frustrations, heart-piercing anguish, and the
gut-wrenching sadness that comes with being a child?

*Sometimes late at night, I try to think back to before
I was a father, to capture how I felt and thought. It
seems so strange and unreal to me now. I hate to think
of myself this way, but looking back I see myself
almost like a cardboard cutout. I was so incredibly
one-dimensional. My kids have taken me on this
nonstop, wild emotional roller-coaster ride. I'm exhausted. It is ten times more work than I ever imagined; there is never a moment's peace, but one
undeniable effect is that I have been changed—transformed. If I was a cardboard cutout figure then, now
I feel like a wide-screen Technicolor version of myself.*

The rewards of empathy are many. We can find ourselves
standing comfortably side by side with our children—even
when we are disciplining them. And we get to revisit all the
emotional turmoil of our youth, but this time with the
clarifying assistance of our adult perspective. It gives us the
power to tame storms and quiet the rumbling insecurities of
youth. At the same time, it heals us like a mythical mineral
bath. You cannot do one without receiving the other.

Last year, we went back to visit my parents for a week. I was standing in the kitchen, talking to my mother and watching my father and son working in the vegetable garden. My father was demonstrating the proper technique—or at least his proper technique—for turning over soil. It reminded me of the endless corrections I had undergone. I'm sure he just felt like he was doing his duty, teaching me "the right way," but I hated it. I felt stupid and grew up convinced that I couldn't do anything right.

When we become fathers, we assume a position of natural authority that will last for nearly two decades. We are bigger, stronger, and wiser than our children. We have the knowledge and experience of countless life lessons, and much of their whirlwind of energy is dedicated to soaking up as much of that precious information as possible. What our children need from us is access to our years of experience. What they do *not* need is a live-in know-it-all. Difficult as this may be sometimes, we need to become comfortable with our role as the elder statesman—without ego involvement and without needing to supply all the answers.

Sometimes it feels I'm walking a tightrope. One minute it's my father, sending me the message that I don't know anything, and a few heartbeats later, it's my child, screaming, "You don't know everything!"

Interestingly enough, between these two unartful and garbled messages, it is our children's angry retort that is most instructive. We *don't* know everything; as a matter of fact, if they had a clue as to how little we *did* know, they wouldn't be angry, they'd be terrified.

We must learn how to provide our children with the information that's necessary and the information that is asked for, without interfering with their sense of wonder and experimentation and without encouraging their natural inclination to believe that we know more than we actually do. We can help them understand, we can coach them in ways to approach problems, we can encourage them to take risks, and we can pass on what wisdom we have gained from our experiences—but it must be an offering, not a demand. Our children don't need us to have answers for every question, they don't need us to be infallible superheroes. They may at times imagine us in this light, but what they really need from us is the benefit of our experience, buttressed by our unconditional love, untainted honesty, unfailing support, and unswerving encouragement.

My father was a bundle of energy. He always seemed to have forty things going on, and whatever he was doing, he would be completely into it. It was fascinating to watch, but it also caused him and me no end of troubles, because if I ever asked for help, he wouldn't just help, he would take over. My science projects became major affairs, with my role being the mad scientist's assistant. I guess what I really learned from that was how to hide things from him. I'd ask my little

sister for help in math before I'd let on to my dad that
I was having trouble. I just couldn't stand in the face
of his "help."

The best lessons are those learned by oneself. We know this, god how we know this, and yet it is so easy to fall prey to the temptation of always supplying answers. Sometimes it is our own childish need to show that we know the answer: Our child asks a question, and we suddenly feel ourselves back in school, our hand waving frantically in the air: I know! I know the answer! Other times it is just the overwhelming desire to fix the problem.

I love my children so much and I know how difficult
growing up can be, so I just want to sneak them as
much information as I can. There is so much I want
to say, so much pain and heartbreak I could spare
them if only they would listen, if only I could figure
out how to get them to understand. But it seems like
they never want to hear my "wisdom." They roll their
eyes—"here he goes again"—and tune me out.

Unfortunately (or fortunately), life must be lived, and we cannot hand down our wisdom and experience as a complete package. There are ways, however, to use our knowledge to efficiently lead, nudge, entice, and prod our children to their own experiences. By knowing our children very well, by paying close attention to their rapidly changing concerns, we can become reliable and effective coaches. We can encourage them in directions we believe will enrich their lives; anticipate and identify issues that they will need to ponder; help them to analyze situations that seem confusing and to articulate their feelings; and show them how understanding those feelings is the compass that will lead them to seeing more clearly.

We can do all this without supplying the answers and without taking over. In the process, we will add to instead of detract from the self-confidence our children need to meet life's challenges.

When I was very young, I played baseball on the same team as my older brother. He was our best pitcher and hitter. I, on the other hand, was the runt of the team, always stuck out in right field, where I would do the least damage. After one particularly bad game in which I had made a couple of run-scoring errors and done my usual four strikeouts, I was almost in tears. I remember refusing to get into the car to go home. I guess I thought I was punishing myself by walking. Anyway, my mom took my brother home, and my dad walked with me. He didn't lecture me or try to cheer me up. He did, however, tell me a great story about how when he was a little boy, he had single-handedly lost a basketball game for his school team.

When our children run into roadblocks, what they need most from us is understanding and empathy. Because we are so used to solving problems in our working environment, it is very easy for us to just jump to the solution quickly and efficiently. Unfortunately, that approach can undermine instead of help. What's worse, it means losing a golden opportunity to support and connect with our children at the deepest level.

If we are to be good coaches for our children, we need to know when to be supportive, when to prod and encourage, when to advise and analyze, and when to simply offer understanding. At any given moment, there will always be a specific "problem," but in a larger and much more important sense, the real issue our children are grappling with is how to analyze and come up with their own solutions. The specific issues will always sort themselves out—with or without our help; it is the skills and confidence to sort out their own problem that our children really need, and it is there that our energy should be focused.

I was trying to study for this big exam and do child-care duty at the same time. I was parked in front of this playground, with my books spread all over the front seat while my five-year-old daughter and seven-year-old son played. After about half an hour, my daughter came running over to the car, complaining that this boy wouldn't let her go down the slide. I looked over, and there was this kid about her age, parked on top of the slide. I told her that I could sure understand her frustration, but I was pretty sure that between her and her brother they could figure something out, and I went back to studying. I did sneak a peek a little later, however, and there were all three of them sliding away. What was interesting was that while normally she and her brother fought like dogs and cats, for the rest of that day they were like the best of buddies.

Not surprisingly, at the heart of good coaching is feeling. We need to understand and empathize with our children's feelings. Often that is all they need from us. Growing up can be very frustrating. Our children must feel as though they are navigating through treacherous and mystifying waters without any of the tools or resources they need to succeed. What they require more than anything is for us to provide the emotional safety net that will give them the strength and courage to persevere. They need to be able to rely upon us to support them without judgment when they falter, to encourage and assure them when they grow timid or confused, and to assist and advise them when they ask for it.

We moved from a small town to a big city the summer before I entered high school. I was going from a junior high school with less than two hundred students to a high school with more than four thousand. I was petrified and trying very hard not to show it. A few days before school started, my dad took me down to the high school and we just walked around the campus for a couple of hours. There were people running all over—teachers, janitors, cafeteria workers—and my father went out of his way to approach quite a number of them. He would very casually let drop that we were new to town and that I would be a freshman there that year. One teacher we met gave us an insider's tour, telling me where the seniors hung out and just making it all sound pretty tame and unintimidating.

When the first day of school rolled around, I wasn't nearly as nervous as I thought I'd be. It was really reassuring to walk down halls that I had been down with my father just a couple of days before. When I got to my home room, my teacher was the man who had given us the tour. He smiled at me and welcomed me by name. My dad has always denied setting that up, but I'm still not sure.

Living life to the fullest requires taking risks. On one level, this is completely obvious: Just identifying a need raises the distinct possibility that we won't be able to satisfy it. Ask a favor and we risk being turned down. Ask for a date and risk rejection. Start a new business and risk financial ruin. Everything from the most inconsequential to the most important things in life requires us to put ourselves, our money, our ego, our heart, and our physical well-being at risk. Yet we live in a society that has become so focused on avoiding risk taking that it can be easy to forget how important it is to help our children develop the skill and courage to take risks.

Sometimes it scares me how obsessed we have become about "security." I'm terrified that my children will be

*too afraid to do the things they need to do to be happy
and successful in their lives. I've tried, largely by
example, to let them see that you just can't compro-
mise, you can't play it safe when it comes to what you
really want and believe.*

Traditionally, in almost every culture, the role of teaching
risk-taking behavior has fallen to fathers. From the earliest
memories of our species, we have had to be prepared to risk
everything to protect our children. Fathers taught children
how to make their way in the wild, how to recognize dangers
without letting those dangers hinder them from accom-
plishing their tasks. So also it is today. The specific dangers
might have changed from wild animals and enemy tribes to
bullies and busy streets, but the most debilitating danger
remains the same: pervasive, overwhelming, self-defeating
fear. It is our job to teach our children to be fearless.

One of the best ways to teach them how to evaluate new
situations, to understand how much risk is reasonable, and
to be comfortable and unintimidated, even in completely
foreign territory, is to give them a guided tour.

*When I was six, my father took me wilderness camp-
ing. The preparations were great fun—planning out
meals, what we needed to pack, looking over the map
of the wilderness area. We had rented a little backpack
for me, and he showed me how to adjust all the straps
and tie on my sleeping bag. The first day out, he
showed me how to use a compass and a topographical*

map and then appointed me the "guide." It was incredible fun until that first night. There we were, sitting around our camp stove cooking dinner, and it just got darker and darker and darker. I don't think I've ever seen it so dark. Then I started hearing all the night sounds. By time dinner was ready, I was so scared I was practically in his lap.

After dinner, he put his arm around me and pointed out some of the constellations in the sky. I remember being amazed when I looked up at how many stars there were up there. Every now and then, he'd identify the animal sounds we could hear and reassure me that they were more afraid of us than I was of them. I still remember that trip so clearly, I think partly because it was such a daring adventure for me and he helped me be not so scared.

We need to expand their worlds. Some parents are so worried about protecting their children that they end up with children who are seriously handicapped. Inadvertently we accomplish what the ancient Chinese did purposefully in the practice of binding girls' feet—we wrap them in such tight protection that they end up hobbling through life, afraid to take any risks whatsoever.

Expose your children to the real world. Have them sort through their clothes and toys and go with you to deliver them to a local charity. Take them with you to work or on business trips.

Involve them with money. Two findings repeatedly

surface from study after study: How to deal with money is one of the biggest issues of anxiety and contention among couples; and children who grew up in families that exposed them to economic issues turned out to be the best managers of business. This is not surprising; what is surprising is how many parents continue to keep their children almost completely ignorant of real economic issues. Give your younger children an allowance for chores done around the house and yard; then make a special shopping trip so they can spend the money as they choose. Involve older kids in family financing; have them participate in planning a family vacation, complete with weighing different options that have to fit into an overall vacation budget. Let teenagers help balance the checkbook and see what groceries, gas, and insurance cost; talk to them about credit cards and about saving for college. If you own a business, expose them to the financial side as well as utilizing their labor.

When my daughter was twelve, she really wanted a fancy ten-speed bike, and I said I'd pay half if she earned the other half. So she came up with what she thought was a great plan and made up a handful of flyers, advertising yard work. She really undercut the market and ended up with six regular jobs. At first, she was ecstatic and had dreams of all this money piling up. Fairly soon, she had enough for the bicycle, but she hardly ever had a chance to ride it because between school and working on all those yards, there was little time left.

She lasted for a couple of months and then she really wanted to quit, so she told one of her customers, this old grumpy man who was never satisfied anyway, that her father ordered her to quit because it was cutting into her schoolwork. Needless to say, it got back to me. I sat her down and asked what she thought she was going to accomplish by lying. She tried diversion, weaseling around for a while about working too much and how it really was cutting into her schoolwork, but I kept looking at her like, "Nope, wrong answer." She finally had to admit that she just wanted to quit and was looking for an easy way out.

I told her there was no easy way out. She could quit if that was what she decided she needed to do, but she had to be honest about it and willing to accept the consequences, which in this case meant it was pretty unlikely that any of them would hire her the next time she wanted to make some money. She thought about it and ended up quitting three of the jobs and keeping the other three.

When our children get themselves in over their head, we are almost always tempted to dive in and come to the rescue. But in so doing, we rob them of the opportunity to grow that the moment of crisis presents. One of the least-discussed secrets of life is that it is precisely in such moments—when we are forced to face the very thing that appears to be the most difficult to face—that true growth and transformation can take place.

Rescuing our children prematurely can cripple them just as surely as neglect or overprotection. We need to provide them the opportunity—the benediction—to learn how to solve their own problems. In the long run, this gift will be the most valuable skill we can teach them.

This is such a difficult assignment: to stand there, knowing that you could step in and alleviate the immediate pain, yet also knowing that by doing so you would do more damage than good. It is a delicate balance that we must maintain and always be conscious of. Good fathering does not stem purely out of instinct, simply because we love our children. We need to apply all our love, all our strength, and all our analytical skills in this endeavor.

I grew up in a really small town, and my summer salvation was playing league baseball. Each year at the beginning of summer, they had two tryout days, and you had to attend one of them to get on a team. When I was thirteen, I missed the first day for some reason. Shortly afterward, my cousins invited me to go to a baseball game between the Pirates and the Cardinals. I rarely ever went to major-league games, because the nearest park was four hours away, so this was a big deal. Unfortunately, it was the same day as the last tryout.

I went to the game and had a great time, but the price was an unbelievably long and boring summer. All my friends were playing baseball, and I was stewing in the stands. At one point, I got really upset and

said to my father something like, "Why did you let me
do that?" He said he figured I was old enough to make
my own mistakes.

Our mistakes are frequently our best teachers. They give us
the hard-to-dismiss feedback we need to do better next time.
Helping our children become comfortable making mistakes
is an important and surprisingly difficult task. From the
earliest moments of their lives, our children are constantly
undertaking what seems to them to be a vast mountain range
of challenges. From gaining basic control over their physical
movements to speaking, reading, writing, and thinking
systematically, it feels to them as though they are constantly
struggling with things that everyone else (adults) seems to be
able to do easily and perfectly.

One of the most surprising and difficult things for me
was watching my son grapple with making mistakes.
It made him nuts. He wanted to do everything per-
fectly. He got upset if he missed a question on a test or
if he made an error playing baseball—it was like he felt
that his next mistake might be fatal. I tried and tried
to convince him that it was no big deal, that we all
make mistakes, but for the longest time he wasn't
having any of it.

From the child's position, it is easy to become obsessed with
"doing it right" and to feel like complete a failure for making
a mistake. We need to give our children room to trip and fall,

but we also need to give them plenty of reassurance that
bloopers, blunders, and pratfalls are the stuff that life is
made of.

*My father tried to teach me how to play golf when I
was about eight. For some reason, I thought I should
have been able to hit the ball perfectly after a few
weeks' practice. The first time he ever took me out on
the course, I hit the first shot off the tee about five feet
and threw my golf club about fifteen feet. That was
the end of my first round of golf. Dad sat me down and
told me there were three kinds of mistakes: the kind
you expect—like mis-hitting a golf ball; the kind you
make out of ignorance or inexperience—like talking
when someone else is hitting, because no one ever told
you that you shouldn't; and the kind you will be held
responsible for because you should know better and
you should be able to avoid them—like throwing your
club. I was grounded for a week, but I never threw
another club.*

There are mistakes and then there are mistakes. Like just
about every other aspect of fathering, judging which mistakes to welcome and make your children comfortable with,
which ones to frame as an acceptable one-time learning
experience, and which ones to be seriously concerned about
takes some doing. It is part and parcel of the daily balancing
act of fathering. We need to push and challenge, encourage
and reassure, support and comfort, set limits and impose

consequences, and do it all within the ever-changing and evolving context of each child's personality. Last, and perhaps most important of all, we need to remember that we too make mistakes, and, ultimately, that just may be the best lesson of all.

A few years ago, I finally got around to telling my father that I now understood a little of what he must have gone through. He dug this yellowed folder out of a file cabinet and showed me these two artifacts of my youth. The first was something I had written when I was in the third grade about how my dad was the best person in the whole universe and that he knew practically everything. The second one was an angry letter I had sent him from college, during the height of my separations spasms, accusing him of being the most inconsiderate and dense father in the world.

There are very few jobs imaginable for which the job description changes so radically over time. When our children are young, they assume that we know everything; and from that lofty position, most of our energy can be focused on giving them the emotional support and encouragement they need—praising their efforts, listening to their ideas, creating opportunities for them to have some power, even if it's just over what's for dinner, what books to read, or which games to play. The heart of our attention is on their feelings, trying to help them understand and articulate the raw flood of emotions powering their little bodies.

As they grow older and begin to suspect that we aren't so smart after all, the balance begins to shift. As always, their feelings are the foundation from which we must begin, but increasingly they will demand that we focus more and more on the substance of things. This can be a very delicate dance, as their budding debating style sometimes veers into wildly illogical loops. We need to be skillful at honoring their feelings—dealing honestly and straightforwardly with their emerging intellects, without making them feel foolish, and encouraging them to stretch their minds and souls farther outward.

Eventually, sometimes gradually and sometimes with jarring suddenness, we are bumped off the paternal pedestal. No matter how much we might have protested our fallibility, exposed our stumblings, and apologized for our mistakes, the time will come when our children finally realize that we aren't the paragons of virtue and intelligence they once assumed we were. And when that time comes, they will frequently be angry at us. It may feel unfair, and in some ways it undoubtedly will be, but we can take comfort in the knowledge that it is an essential milestone in our children's initiation into adulthood. It is also the final transformation necessary to allow us to properly coach and counsel our young adults as they take their first tentative steps into the world of their future.

My sixteen-year-old daughter, who lives with her mother, called me the other day to tell me a dream she had. In her dream, she was in this very exotic village.

In that village were many small shops with all manner of different goods for sale. She said that as she wandered through the village and looked at all the amazing things in the shops, she realized that she could have anything she wanted, because her father owned all the stores. It made her feel very happy, but she also said that the only thing she actually took was a set of beautiful luggage.

After telling me the dream, she asked me what I thought it meant. I told her I didn't think I should be the one to interpret this dream for her because I thought it was about me. She said she already knew that and persisted. I told her that the village was the world she was about to step into—a very beautiful, magical, and welcoming place. And that while she knew there were many presents she could take from me, the only one she needed was the luggage. As I finished, my voice was wavering with emotion and I told her that a father's job is to provide his children with good luggage.

We talked for a while longer, and I ended the call as I always have, saying, "I love you, sweetheart." She answered, "I love you too, Dad, and Dad, thanks for the luggage."

One of the first things that strikes a man when he becomes a father is the terrifying concern that something might happen to his child. For the rest of our life, the security of our children will be uppermost in our mind. We can weave a strong safety net with our emotional support and we can guide and protect them as they are growing, but ultimately the only real security our children will have is the skill and self-confidence to know that they can handle whatever comes along.

Helping them to acquire those skills, to build a solid foundation of self-esteem, is our sacred task as fathers, a commitment of the deepest and most unconditional love. It binds us to them with such intense power that finally, when the time is right, we can let them go.

Chapter 9

Fathering Across Distance

One evening, I was working late and had just gotten off the phone with my daughter. She sounded kind of down in the dumps, so I went out to the Xerox machine, made a copy of my face—all distorted and funny looking—and faxed it to her at my home fax number with a little love note attached. That really cheered her up. Last week, I was in her room, trying to find a magazine she had borrowed from me and I saw this big, fat file folder full of all the faxes I have sent her since then. It was quite a feeling.

Distance appears to be the one constant in most father/child relationships. We are separated by work: all day and late nights at the office; jobs such as with the airlines, regional sales, or the military, that take us away on a regular basis; or simply too many hours and too many obligations. Many of us are separated by divorce—living in different homes and different cities. This distance in time and space can corrode the bonds we work so hard to establish with our children. Ultimately, as a society, we need to find ways to lessen the pressures pulling us apart, but in the interim, we as individuals need to find more effective ways to bridge the distance we cannot avoid.

My father disappeared from my life when I was seven. He'd send birthday cards and a Christmas present, but for all practical purposes, he was nonexistent. I used to make up all these stories in my mind about what he was doing and why he never called or came to visit. When I was thirty-three, he just showed up one day. He was sick and wanted me to know that he was sorry he'd been such a lousy father. I asked him why he had disappeared, and he said it was the only way he knew to stop the pain. I wanted to forgive him but I didn't know how.

Divorce can be extremely painful, massively disrupting, gut-wrenchingly difficult, and absolutely terrifying as well as liberating and life-transforming. It can be many things, but we need to do everything in our power to make sure that it does not mean abandoning our children. There is no excuse for our offspring becoming victims of our decisions, no excuse for using our children as weapons, and no excuse for exposing our children to such an ugly whirlwind of trauma and accusations that we feel like fleeing just to protect the innocent bystanders. And there is no excuse for running away from our children, no matter how difficult and painful it gets.

> *I've talked to a lot of divorced dads, and I realize just how lucky I've been. Both my daughter and I are big-time talkers. Moving to an apartment was hard, but from the beginning, I would talk to my daughter every day on the phone. Once when she was still quite young, she ran out of things to say, but she wasn't ready to stop talking to Daddy, so she opened up a cupboard and described the entire contents to me. By the time she hung up, I was trying so hard not to laugh out loud, I was in tears.*

No matter how artfully we manage the separation, divorce almost always presents a difficult challenge for fathers—how to maintain and strengthen our connections with our children from a distance. The number of fathers being granted primary custody has risen of late, but it is and in the foreseeable future almost certainly will remain the exception rather than the rule. What that means is that for most fathers, one consequence of divorce is the urgent need to rebuild and redefine the pathways to and from our children's hearts.

Most marriages begin filled with love soaring on the

wings of hope. When they end, the vast distance we plunge seems to bring out the worst in us. It is so difficult to be compassionate when we want to blame someone else for the terrible pain, so hard to even be civil when in each interaction we can feel the residue of every disappointment, every argument, every betrayal. These are the issues we must work out, and hopefully in the process become better people— more patient, more understanding, more forgiving, and more accepting. But when there are children in the line of fire, we do not have the luxury to vent first and heal later. Our first concern should be protecting our children from our own temporary insanity.

It was fairly early after our breakup, and it seemed like every time we talked, it would deteriorate into a screaming match. One day she had called me, demanding that I bring my daughter back five hours early because she had plans that evening. I found myself screaming at her over the telephone right in front of my daughter. When I hung up the phone, I saw the look in her eyes and felt about two inches high. It really didn't matter who was the most wrong; we were both being complete jerks. That was it. I just decided I would never respond that way again. At the very least, my daughter deserved to have one of her parents act like a mature adult.

If we are going to teach our children anything about how to live, it will not be as a result of all the great speeches we give, but by the example we set. And there is no nexus of their lives where they will be more sensitized toward how we behave than with their mother. If, in the midst of all the emotional turmoil that surrounds the ending of a relationship, we can manage to treat her with respect and dignity—regardless of her behavior—it will establish a strong foundation to build upon. A foundation we will need, because as divorced fathers, our relationship with our children will change dramatically.

> *By the time we finally realized that our marriage was over, there wasn't anything left between us except the children. What I will always be thankful for is that throughout the entire awkward and painful process of disentanglement, we were both very careful to avoid doing anything to affect the relationship of either one of us with our children. It was as if the sole remaining thing we had was a mutual love for our children and a mutual understanding of how important it was to them to have a strong relationship with both their parents.*

When love comes undone between two adults, it is the perfect time to acknowledge and respect the power and importance of each parent's love for his or her children. If we love our children, we must respect their needs and their love of others. That mutual respect can become the basis for a caring and compassionate cooperation between us and our former spouse.

When I think back to the breakup, I am really proud of how we managed it. We were so mismatched it wasn't funny; and when we were alone, we said some really horrible things to each other, but we were both so terrified of hurting the kids that out of sheer terror we managed to do a pretty good job of working through things. We sat them down and together explained that we both loved them very much, that Daddy was going to move to a different house but that we would always both be their parents and would always be there for them.

Although divorce creates distance, it needn't create absence. For many fathers, it is the trauma of divorce, the forced confrontation with their deepest feelings, that galvanizes them into a more powerfully connected relationship to their children.

At first I didn't know what to do. I had never realized how different it was going to be not having them there every night. For me, it made a huge difference, because I have never been much of a talker. My relationship with my kids was always so physical—roughhousing, clowning around, daily hugs. Suddenly, I was stuck at the end of a telephone. For about six months, things just sort of drifted, and then I realized that I had to do something or I was going to lose them. I borrowed a video recorder from a friend and made a five-minute, off-the-wall, narrated tape of my new apartment.

That did it; they went nuts. That Christmas, I bought two video recorders—one for them and one for me. We probably have enough footage by now to make three full-length movies.

Fathering across a distance requires tremendous commitment. It is all too easy to let things drift. There are no good, healthy models, we don't have great support systems for doing this, we are often obstructed or at least not always encouraged by our ex-wife, and society itself seems to reinforce the message that fathers just aren't that important.

At times when I begin to feel that it's easier to let go, I've learned it's good to dig down and rely on one of those old-fashioned male characteristics—pure stubbornness. Nothing, but nothing is going to stop me from having the kind of relationship I need with my children. If one approach doesn't work, I try another and another and another.

With my oldest daughter, the distance never seemed to matter. I called her every other day, and it was like one long continuous conversation. It just came easily. With my second daughter, she'd be really excited when she first got on the phone, but then she'd just stumble into silence. It's like between the two of us, we couldn't keep a conversation going for more than a few minutes.

There are no easy answers—we are literally making it up on the fly. Some of us find telephones a lifesaver whereas others of us can barely manage a few sentences before we grind to a halt. At the same time, our children are all unique. What they need from us and how they can receive it will vary from child to child and from year to year.

One night, I was working late at the office on this really boring case. I was "propounding interrogatories," which is a fancy way of saying I was writing page after page of ludicrous questions that the other side in this lawsuit was going to have to answer. I called and talked to my daughter for a few minutes, and she made some comment about one of her friends, but then I couldn't get her to explain what she meant. After I hung up, I was thinking about her and I started "editing" my interrogatories to make them funny. Then I rewrote them, directing them to her about this friend that she was obviously miffed at. It was the most fun I've ever had doing interrogatories and I dropped them in the mail the next day.

A week later, I got a long, detailed written response with more information about her relationship to this particular friend than I could ever have gotten out of her on the telephone. I was totally hooked. Since then we have traded sets of questions for six years, sometimes very detailed and serious questions, sometimes completely off-the-wall questions. One of my favorite was when I sent her as a tongue-in-cheek high-school

graduation question, "What is the meaning of life?"
She wrote back, "To answer the next set of questions."

Ultimately, for a father living apart from his children, the issue is not absence, for no matter how painful, that is something we can all adjust to. The real issue is presence: how to be, consistently and meaningfully, a presence in our children's lives.

I'm not terribly good on the telephone—it's usually, "Hi, how are things?" a couple minutes of chit-chat, "I love you," and good-bye. But they know that I will be there Friday, and we'll spend the weekend together. The weekend is the time we are together, and nothing is going to get in the way of that. Sometimes my friends think I'm weird because I am so inflexible about my weekends, but that is how I let my children know how important they are to me.

One part of creating that presence is reminding them, in whatever way works, just how important they are. It is the articulated, expressed, demonstrated statement of our own need—I love you unconditionally because you are my child, and at the very depth of my soul I need to be as good a father to you as I possibly can because I need you in my life.

Three years after we split up, my ex-wife moved five hundred miles away. It really made it difficult. The first thing I did was buy a new car—I was not going to let bad weather stand in the way of seeing my son as often as I possibly could. The second thing I did was to buy a block of round-trip airline tickets for him to use. By the time he was twelve, he had more frequent flyer miles than most businessmen I know. And I had more miles on my car than anyone else in the country.

Being a father by definition requires sacrifice. But any seasoned father can tell you that no matter how much sacrifice is required, the rewards are always greater.

My ex-wife lived three hundred miles away. One night, I had driven down to pick up my kids and was on the way back to my house for the week. It was around three o'clock in the morning; I was racing against exhaustion and got pulled over by a highway patrolman. My five-year-old son was sound asleep in the backseat and my three-year-old daughter was asleep in the front seat. I remember there was an extraordinary full moon shining down on her face. This tough-guy cop walked up to my window and just melted. He knew instantly what was happening. He just stood there for a few minutes, looking at my sleeping kids, and then said, "God, they are beautiful—slow down, OK?" It's the only ticket I've ever gotten out of.

One of the most difficult things for fathers to do is turn to other fathers for support. We know the reasons: our diffi-

culty with articulating and expressing emotions, our com-
petitiveness, our pride, our raw inexperience in this arena. It
is probably our greatest weakness, because it forces each one
of us to reinvent fathering all over again. Particularly when
we are struggling with the distance created by divorce, we
need to make a concerted effort to integrate that part of our
life as a father with our life as a man.

> *I have a friend I've known for twenty years. When we*
> *were younger, we hung around together, we both got*
> *married and had kids, and then we both got divorced.*
> *We still see each other fairly regularly. When we get*
> *together, we talk about sports and current events and*
> *sometimes work-related issues. A few months ago, we*
> *were at a baseball game and he was brooding about*
> *something. Well, one thing lead to another, and it*
> *turned out his fifteen-year-old daughter who lives*
> *with her mother had gotten pregnant, and he was*
> *really upset because he felt like he had not done a good*
> *enough job keeping himself firmly in her life.*
>
> *We spent the entire afternoon talking about our*
> *kids and the problems and issues we were trying to*
> *come to grips with about being fathers. It was really a*
> *wonderful experience, and later that night I got to*
> *thinking and realized that I had never—and I mean*
> *never—talked about these things to anyone before.*
> *There was a part of my mind that just couldn't believe*
> *it. Here I was with two kids of my own and two*
> *stepchildren—all already well into their teens—and I*

hadn't talked about being a father to anyone. It's enough to make me believe men must have portions of our brains that just lock up sometimes.

I also realized after talking to my friend that he had let his daughter down, but it wasn't because he didn't love her and it wasn't because he didn't want to be bothered; it was because he didn't know what to do. He didn't have a clue how to make himself an important part of her life from two hundred miles away.

What we need to do is anything and everything that works to pry open their hearts. And that means searching for the avenues that lead most directly into each of our children's lives.

I was having a terrible time with my son. I'd call and talk to him, and within minutes he'd be down to one-word answers to my increasingly frantic questions. I just couldn't get through to him. One day, I was talking to a friend about how frustrating it was with my son so far away and me feeling so helpless. She asked me if I ever wrote him letters. The answer was no; it never occurred to me since the telephone seemed so much easier. I had nothing to lose, so that night I went home and wrote him a long letter. I just wrote about how I was doing and about how worried I was about him.

A week later, I got this exquisite letter (it had my

*name on the address and then after my name in
parentheses it said "Dad"). All those frustrating phone
calls, and suddenly here in this letter he was shining
through in living color. I couldn't believe it. My first
reaction was to reach for the phone but I stopped
myself just in time. We've been writing back and forth
for three years now, and it's really incredible. When
we get together every other month, it's like we've never
been apart.*

What works for one child won't necessarily work for another, so we need to become masters of alternative forms of
communication. It's up to us to adjust to our children's
needs, not vice versa. The better we can tailor our approach
to the individual communication styles of our children, the
more we will become a vibrant force in their lives.

*My relationship with my daughter has gone through
loops that are hard to believe. We live on opposite
coasts, so it's difficult to get together anywhere near as
much as we both want to, but I have been absolutely
insistent on being a real and functioning part of her
daily life. It's been great, but it's also been a real ride.
Once, right after getting off the phone with her, I was
so upset I drove to the airport and caught the next
flight to California. It was probably an overreaction,
but she got the point: nothing was going to stand in
the way of our relationship, including three thousand
miles of cornfields and desert.*

Sometimes we need to stretch the boundaries of imagination in order to be a constant force in our children's lives. They come in so many different configurations, and by virtue of having become a father, it is now our responsibility—not theirs—to figure out just what is necessary in order to get through.

> *When my son hit puberty, he turned into a classic computer techno-nerd. I couldn't get him to stay on the telephone for more than five minutes, and when he was on the telephone, I couldn't get him to talk about anything but "Myst" and other computer minutiae. I had no choice. Against all my instincts, I went out and bought a state-of-the-art multimedia computer and enlisted the help of a wonderful woman who knows everything about computers.*
>
> *The best part was my first e-mail message to my son. He didn't even know I had a computer, and all of a sudden he has this mysterious e-mail message. I was stretching my technological capacity to the max, but it was like magic—suddenly we had a common language and, more importantly, a common medium. I doubt that many e-mail users save every message, but I have three disks full of my son's e-mail, and someday, when he is a father, I'm going to give them to him.*

Distance between children and fathers can be measured in miles, but also in heartbeats. Both kinds of distance have consequences, but ultimately the distance we cannot compensate for, the kind that leaves lasting wounds, is emotional distance. It is the thunderous silence of a broken connection, the unmistakable absence of something we *know* should be there, the unbearable strain of waiting for a feeling that never comes. And that can happen no matter where you live.

> *My parents "stayed together for the kids." It was an absolutely hellish experience. At first they fought, but eventually they didn't even care enough to fight. My mom poured all her energy, love, loneliness, and sadness into us, and my father ignored us completely. It was like we weren't even there.*

Emotional distance can begin in the next room or the next city. And although there are extreme cases where that distance appears as a purposefully erected barrier, it is almost always an unintended and unwanted impediment. Perhaps it stems from our biological position of beginning from the "outside," but at times it appears as though there is a gravitational force pulling us away from a deep emotional bond with our children. If we live our life without thinking about it, without paying close attention to what kind of father we want to be, the distance can seep into the cracks and expand until one day we find ourselves on the other side of a wide and empty chasm.

For most fathers, even if we live with our children, the gravest danger is work. There are so many forces pushing us toward spending more and more time at work that we end up spending long hours away from home, bringing work back from the office, and working weekends and evenings. Many of us have jobs that take us away for days, weeks, or even, particularly for military fathers, months at a time.

> *My wife got pregnant and we got married. From day one it was tough; there was so little money, then my son got sick. I ended up working two jobs to keep us afloat, and when I was home, I was so tired I'd sit in front of the television like a zombie. One day—my son was four—I was trying to be playful and I said something to him, and he started crying. It was like being hit right between the eyes with hammer—I realized that on some level, we were almost strangers.*

The struggle to balance work and our kids is a difficult one, because for the most part there is nothing subtle about work pressures. Bills need to be paid, our bosses or our businesses demand more and more time and concentration. On the other hand, there is the soft and gentle feel of our connection to our children. It is frighteningly easy to lose track of that subtle feel, to let it slip away in the stress of keeping up on the job front. It is just as easy in the concentrated focus of work to lose track altogether of the markedly different patterns and rhythms of our children's lives.

> *I'm an airline pilot and am often away for days at a time. I came home from work one day to find a police officer sitting in my living room with my wife. At first,*

I was terrified that one of my children had been in an accident. I found out that my daughter had been arrested for joyriding. It was such a strange rush of feelings, first the unbelievable relief, then complete disbelief, followed by the frightening realization that I didn't really know who my daughter was. That night when I tried to talk to her, she broke down crying. All she could say was, "You're never here and when you are here, I see you and you never see me, you never see me . . . you don't care."

That was it. I could not for my life figure out how I had gotten there, but just the sight of my daughter crying like that, knowing that she was at least halfway right, I realized that somewhere I had really screwed up and I was going to find a way to let her know that I care about her more than almost anything in the world.

Sometimes, the combination of physical proximity and emotional distance is the most painful arrangement of all. There are plenty of fathers living in different homes who don't know how to make themselves a strong emotional presence in their children's lives. But it can be much more difficult for our children to deal with when they must physically experience that painful distance every single day.

I was working long hours at my job and also helping my wife start a business. I worked ten hours a day, seven days a week. I remember all the weekends my

*daughter would literally beg me to pay attention to her
for even ten minutes, but I remember it through a fog.
It was like I was on this treadmill that I couldn't stop
and I couldn't get off of. Looking back from where I am
today, it's hard for me to understand how I could not
have heard the cry in her voice and how I could not
have found some way to give her the time she needed.*

Upon reflection, it's a wonder that so many of us—wonderfully skilled at figuring out the most intricate logical problems—can be so incredibly dense about something so crucially important to us as our children.

*My children were in school, my daughter in second
grade and my son in kindergarten, when my wife was
seriously injured in a car accident. By the time I got
word, school had been out for hours. I rushed home,
and they were sitting in the living room, looking like
frightened animals. They didn't even know their mother
was in the hospital; all they knew was that she wasn't
there and they didn't know how to reach me. What
had I been thinking?*

*When things settled down, we had a little telephone communications seminar. I made them memorize my office number, my pager, and my calling card
so they could call me from anywhere. Then we devised
a series of codes for the pager: 111 for "I really, really,
need to talk to you"; 222 for "Boy, I'd sure like to talk
to you if possible"; and 333 for "Call me—I'm bored."*

Then my daughter came up with a fourth code, "XOXOXO" for "I love you, Daddy." Boy, do I love getting those XOXOXO pages!

Making sure your children can reach you is much more than a good emergency safeguard. It is the establishment of an invisible and unbreakable connection—it lets them know that even in the midst of your busy schedule, they have access because they are important.

A couple of years ago, I was leaving for a five-day business trip and it really bothered me that I would miss reading them a good-night story. So I taped a story for each night I was gone, and when it was bedtime, my wife pulled out the tape recorder and played the story. They loved it. Recently, we've gotten really high-tech—we use the video cam so they get to hear my voice and see me, too.

Our children should be constantly reminded of how important to us our connection to them is. And the different ways available to us to do this are unlimited.

Before I leave town, I hide a whole series of funny love notes all over the house. Then at night when I call, I give my kids clues, and they tear off in search of Dad's hidden treasures. They love it, and it makes me feel like I'm still with them in some way.

In strengthening our connection to our children while at work, one of the things that's important is that we stop drawing such hard-and-fast lines between "work" and "home." We need to make room in our working lives for our children, bringing them to work occasionally, communicating with them from work on a regular basis, or simply taking some time each working day to wonder where they are and what they are doing. Just opening those new channels binds us closer together and creates surprising possibilities.

> *I work in San Francisco about two blocks from the Exploratorium, which is an incredibly neat hands-on science museum. One day, my son was on a field trip to the Exploratorium, and in the middle of the day, I remembered he would be there. So I rushed down and sure enough I could see some of his classmates running around. They have this winding tube-like thing that you crawl into; it's pitch black inside with all these different textures you have to crawl across. Thanks to one of his friends letting me take cuts, I managed to sneak in right after him. We were both oohing and aahing over all the different feels, and when I popped out the end, his face lit up like neon sign.*

Our emotional connection to our children is like an invisible umbilical cord. We need to maintain a constant flow of nourishment between us. And whether we live in the same house or thousands of miles away, the key ingredient is time.

Not physical presence, but real, focused, emotionally present time.

> *I grew up in a home where nobody knew how to be with or talk to anyone else. Here I am, decades later, and it's the same thing. My parents want me to visit, they want me to bring over the grandchildren, but when I show up, we end up spending the whole day sitting in front of the television.*

True presence, real time, is when we are fully emotionally engaged. It is when we can see our children from a state of wonder and enjoyment. It can take place in their physical presence, while talking to them on the telephone, or when writing them a letter. No matter how we accomplish it, it bathes and energizes them with a shower of our undivided love and attention.

> *I saw my father only twice a month, but he was far and away the most important influence in my life, because I always felt like he was thinking about me. The more busy he was, the more careful he was to make sure to call or send a postcard—just somehow to let me know I was on his mind. I don't even know how to describe it. No matter what was going on, in hundreds of really small ways, he always made me feel like I was incredibly important to him, that what I thought and felt was more important than anything else he could be*

*doing. Once he called me from the showroom of an
auto dealer; he was buying a new car and he wanted
to know if I thought the dark green or dark blue one
would fit him better.*

True presence, real quality time, does not have to do with
what we are doing or where we are, but *how* we are doing it.
When we are emotionally available to our children—wide
open to whatever they need, welcoming and supportive of
wherever they are—the easy and natural way of being forges
the most pure and unbreakable bonds. It is so simple and yet
so hard to remember.

*It was just a regular day and, as usual, I was tired and
wanted to rest every cell in my body. I was reading the
newspaper, and my daughter was standing beside my
chair, picking at me—pulling on my leg, whining in my
ear—it felt like the buzz of a mosquito. Then I looked
down and somehow I could see how hard she was
trying to get me to acknowledge her and it almost
broke my heart.*

With all our adult distractions, with all the pressures and
obligations tugging for attention, it is easy for us to drift
away, to compartmentalize our mind like a multitasking
computer. One part thinking about a problem at work, one
part worrying over how we are going to get the bills under
control, another part trying to imagine some free time where
we can relax, and still another part answering our children's

questions. To our children, however, that particle of attention feels exactly like what it is—mental crumbs—and it feeds the distance between us.

My father would sit there, reading his newspaper and carrying on these conversations without ever looking up. He would actually call me by my brother's name or answer questions we hadn't asked. In a way it was funny, and we used to purposefully ask weird questions to see what he would say. But basically, it wasn't very funny at all; it was like living with a not-very-bright robot.

We need to try very hard to be present with them whenever we can, and if that is not possible, at least explain to them why. When you live a life that is packed to overflowing, you need to become proficient at twisting time to your needs. One way to stamp time with a special intensity is to be powerfully present.

Another way is to make use of stolen time. We all remember with exquisite joy the feeling of playing hooky—stealing time away from what we are supposed to be doing. Stolen time comes out of nowhere—it surprises and delights. Stolen time stretches out so that a few hours can seem wonderfully long. Stolen time is pure luxury; it exists solely for us to savor. When we share our stolen time with our children, we invite them into an exceedingly intimate and magical world, where our relationship to them is all that exists.

As a divorced father, I've always gone out of my way
to try to create surprising times with my daughter.
Once, I took a day off work, flew to Chicago, pulled her
out of school, and we spent the day at a Cubs game.
Another time, I drove a couple hundred miles out of
my way and took her out for a kid's night on the town
on a school night!

Whether we live in separate cities, are off on submarines for
months at a time, or simply work too much, there is a very
simple truth we need to incorporate in our fathering: distance is measured in neither miles, nor minutes, nor words,
nor touch; the distance that matters is measured in our
children's hearts. Our job is to be there—fully, powerfully,
and always present in their hearts.

Chapter 10

Being There for the Long Haul

What do I know about being a father? I feel like a dumb kid who partied too much and got in over his head. My girlfriend got pregnant because we were having too much fun and not thinking about the consequences. Now here I am, barely old enough to buy my own beer, and I'm supposed to be responsible for a kid. I guess there's an awful lot I need to learn, but I can tell you, the day my daughter was born, the first time I held her, something changed inside me; something just opened up and started to spread throughout my body. I was standing there holding her and I had goose bumps all over.

Being a father stretches us and focuses us in ways we never could have imagined. It binds us to the awesome expanse of time, from the very dawn of creation outward into the dim reaches of the future. And in that vast expanse of time, it offers us, like a sparkling diamond, the sacred intensity of a single moment.

> *I know this is going to sound weird, but I knew the moment my wife conceived. We had decided to have a child and had stopped using birth control, but we weren't exactly being scientific about it. That night when we made love, it was really special and very different. Very loving and tender, but also really playful—we were laughing and giggling and crying. Later that night, I came wide awake, like I had been shaken out of a deep sleep, and I knew at that moment that I was going to be a father.*

It begins with a moment, one of those rare times when we are faced with a decision that will profoundly influence our life, the moment we choose to become a father. While the responsibility and commitment implied in that decision are obvious, perhaps more significant is the subtle but complete alteration of our location on the unfolding map of creation.

In one very important sense, growing up is a process of disconnection—the gradual disentangling from our parents, the slow but inevitable untying of the threads that forcibly hold us to them. We are "grown up" when we successfully disconnect—when we assume full control of and responsibility for our own life. In a very powerful sense, when we first step out of the shelter of our parents' lives, we enter a kind of timeless waiting room, where the past is simply a backdrop and the future seems a promise of endless possibilities.

> *I never wanted to have kids. My childhood wasn't exactly something to write home about, and I didn't emerge from my cocoon with all the pieces in the right places. I knew I was pretty screwed up and I didn't want the responsibility of passing any of that garbage onto a new generation. I married fairly late and not surprisingly picked a woman who was very emotionally repressed. We were safely headed toward a long, boring, loveless, childless marriage, and then she got pregnant and insisted on having the baby. That was the end of our marriage. What I was completely unprepared for was how much my son would change my life.*

Perhaps what is most frightening at this juncture in our life—when we are just beginning to exercise the skills necessary to control our own destiny—is that our options seem virtually limitless. We can dive into a traditional career path or retreat into a life of solitude and contemplation. We can experiment wildly with interests and lifestyles or delve deeply into one very specific and narrow area. We can even choose to completely reject the past and abandon any responsibility to the future. In a sense, it is the time of the full blossoming of our inherent free will.

There is this science fiction book called Childhood's
End. *I don't even remember what it was about now,
but the title sure stuck with me, because I was one of
those Peter Pan guys who thought I could stay young
forever just by going out every night and dating a
different woman every week. It all changed so fast I
can hardly remember the details. I met my wife at a
party, four weeks later we were married, and a month
later she was pregnant.*

Yet no matter how it feels, this time is but a moment in our
life. Eventually we begin making choices that alter the
landscape of our life either slowly or swiftly. Deciding to
become a father is one of those choices, and it defines and
expands our personal universe every bit as dramatically as
the primordial big bang defines and expands the larger
universe surrounding us.

As a father, we become a link in a chain that stretches
across time, instantly and irrevocably connected to our
ancestors and our descendants. As fathers, we also become
an integral part of our community, because that is where our
children will live and grow and because it is our responsibility to do whatever we can to ensure that their community
will not only be safe, but alive with possibilities.

And as a father, we are forced to confront the deepest
spiritual meanings of life. Through the act of conception, we
add our seed to the next generation, and in so doing actively
participate in renewing and perpetuating the family of man.
This is not something that can be done without wondering

why, without searching for meaning and a purpose, without being willing to hold ourselves open to ever deeper and more profound insight. For the most part, however, this dramatic change takes place without our awareness, at least initially, because the process of fathering is every bit as much about our own growth and development as it is about our children's. Just as we owe a sacred bond of responsibility to our children, so must we be responsible to our own challenges—as individuals, as members of an extended family and of our local and global community, and as active participants in the wondrous mystery of life.

I never knew my maternal grandfather. He died in the war when my mother was still quite young, and then my grandmother remarried. No one really talked about him. When I graduated from high school, I really wanted to go to music school, but I was afraid to ask my parents, because they weren't into music and I thought they wouldn't understand. When I finally mentioned it, my mother told me that my grandfather had been a concert pianist. I don't know why, but it had a real effect on me. She dug out a bunch of pictures of him that I guess I'd seen at some time, and there was this young guy, who looked like he could have been my fraternal twin, staring back at me.

At times it seems that at the very core, human nature is an exquisite paradox—we search throughout our lifetime to discover and become who we already are. As our children

begin their long search to bring to full fruition their emerging identities, they will be helped enormously by parents
who have honestly and diligently mapped out the common
territory. In this capacity, as map makers for our young
explorers, the most important territory to record and pass on
is that of our own family.

More than any other influence on our life, our family
will distort and contribute to who we are. Through our
genes, through the intense process of socialization, and
through the deepest imprinting of psychological issues, it is
our family—parents, siblings, grandparents, aunts, uncles,
cousins, and extended albeit ill-defined others—who have
the most profound effect on shaping our understanding and
perceptions of all that is around and within us.

*I come from a long line of alcoholics, and that really
gave me second thoughts about having children, but
at the same time, I am really proud of how so many of
my relatives have dealt with it. Our extended family
is this patchwork collection of hard-core drinkers,
reformed alcoholics, and those who had the good sense
to never let one drop pass their lips. On balance, we've
done a pretty good job, and that gives me hope.*

Our family is our hometown, one we pass on to our children.
If we do not prepare them with as much information as we
can about the side streets and back alleys; the hidden
cupboards and secret stairwells; the hopes, dreams, and
tragedies of this intimate place, we will be sending them out

into the world without a map or a compass.

To do this, we need first to do our part. We must face what we have been given—flaws and all—and commit ourselves to passing on the best of what our family has to offer, while trying our damnedest not to perpetuate some of the more damaging themes. That means understanding our own history, untangling the truth from the lies and dispelling the myths and mists that obscure our vision.

> *I hated my father as much as I loved him. He could be the most insensitive S.O.B. you'd ever want to meet. He grew up during the Depression and was really ground down by all the deprivation he had to endure. I guess he decided that to protect me from that fate, he had to make me tough, so he pushed and pushed and pushed—and then he dropped dead of a heart attack when I was a teenager and smack dab in the middle of hating his guts. It took me a very long time to forgive him and still longer to appreciate all the things he had done for me.*

Facing and accepting our roots also means honoring and appreciating the gifts we have been given—regardless of the source—and uncovering the often buried histories, hopes, and dreams of our parents and other family members. We must do this in order to give our children a place to begin, a context within which they can understand from whence they came, to see clearly the forces that have so powerfully influenced their lives.

I've been all over the map on this one. I hate to admit it, but I'd probably qualify as a stereotype. In the sixties, I thought we were going to change the world in a few short years. Then I got completely disenchanted and tried to escape completely. I thought the whole world was going to hell in a hand basket and I wasn't about to bring kids into that mess. Then I re-entered society but only to get what I could get. I figured I could live behind walls and make enough money to make myself comfortable. Now here I am, a member of the PTA, with three kids, recycling bins, and— hopefully—a much more rational and optimistic view of the world.

Being a father means we are responsible for our commu- nity—from the neighborhood we live in to the frightening global threat of ecological devastation. This wounded world, this troubled community of man, is the legacy we pass on to our children. Unfortunately, these already badly damaged goods are in serious danger of spiraling out of control into a hellish oblivion. If we are to honor our responsibility as fathers, if we are to hold our heads high, knowing that we have done our duty without fear, we have no choice but to do whatever we can to instill kindness and compassion into our public institutions and to fight for programs and policies that promote the healing of our community and our world.

I believe we are living in a very critical time, that in some important way, the total sum of our efforts, right here and now, is going to tip the balance one way or the other. I really feel that my responsibility is to do everything I can to make this world a better place. I've always felt that way, and so having children was both an act of faith—that we can succeed—and a very powerful incentive to intensify that effort.

What we have been given is the sum of our forefathers' efforts—their achievements and their failures. What we pass on to our children will bear our mark. No one man can change the direction of history, but each of us, fully embracing our responsibility as fathers, can add our voice, our shoulder, our time, and our effort. When all is said and done, if we have taught our lessons well, our children will rightfully judge us not only by the strength and depth of our connection to them, but by the earnestness of our commitment to the world we pass on to them and by our willingness to seek answers to even the most difficult questions.

My mother died when my kids were still very young. I had a very hard time with it, because part of me was relieved and another part just couldn't accept that she wasn't around anymore. She had been very sick, but throughout her illness, no matter how much pain she was in, she was always very cheery and affectionate with my children. In the midst of all my turmoil, my daughter, who was six, started having nightmares. I realized that I hadn't really talked to her about what had happened, because I didn't really know what to say. She needed answers, and that forced me to at least begin thinking and talking about issues I had always avoided.

For some mysterious reason, one of the most difficult things for men to admit is what we don't know. The larger the ignorance, the more difficult it is for us to face up to. This may explain why we are so good at the very focused and practical things and so uncomfortable in the arena of abstract emotions and unanswerable questions. We can teach our children to throw a baseball, tune up a car, analyze a problem, get from here to there, and balance a checkbook, but asked why we are here, what life is all about, how we know what is right, what love is, and what happens when we die—and we sputter to a halt.

One day when I picked up my daughter from her day-care center, she told me that her teacher had said that her mother and I were bad because we got divorced, and God says you're not supposed to get divorced. Needless to say, I was furious, but in a way, I'm glad it happened, because we ended up having a long conversation about God, right and wrong, individual responsibility, and what it meant to be an imperfect human being. At one point, I said something like, "The God I know . . . ," and she got really excited and said, "Daddy, when did you meet God?"

These are questions we can only speculate about, areas in which there are no answers, only beliefs. Tackling these questions can be an uncomfortable frontier, but we owe it to our children to stake out our territory, no matter how tenuous, no matter how difficult it is for us to explain or justify. Our children deserve to know us—to know who we are and what we believe. We may be wrong, they may disagree, but we owe them the answers we choose to believe in. For these are the answers that give meaning and purpose to our life.

> *Shortly after my son was born, my wife and I separated. She moved out of state more than seven hundred miles away. Every two months, I would travel to see him, but it was a constant struggle. My ex-wife made it so difficult that I was sinking into a dark depression, and I began to question whether anything in my life would ever go right again. It wasn't until he was two years old that I was finally able to get him overnight. The very first day we were together, I took him to visit this huge dam; while we were down inside, an alarm went off, and he was so scared he clung to me like a glove. I picked him up and carried him out while he wrapped himself as tightly around me as possible. From that moment on, we have always been very close.*

In thinking about these larger issues, one thing emerges with striking clarity. It is moments—not days, weeks, or months—

but individual, crystal-clear moments that we remember and cherish, that become for us the symbols, the milestones, the precious content of our life.

> *It seems like such a little thing. I missed an awful lot of my children's growing up, because I was always working. Then suddenly, I was unemployed. I got up the next morning and instead of going to work I walked my two daughters to school. That short walk with their small hands in mine is still so clear in my mind, like it was yesterday.*

We are connected across time, but it is only in the moment that we live. As fathers, we need to find ways to share this simple but profound truth with our children.

> *It was a very lazy Saturday, and my daughter had climbed up onto my lap while I was sitting on the porch, reading the newspaper. She snuggled into a comfortable position, and I thought she had fallen asleep. I put down the paper, closed my arms around her, and just sat there, quietly feeling her heart beat against me, smelling her wonderful little-kid smell all mixed up with the early summer smells coming from the yard. After a few minutes, she looked up at me with this absolutely angelic smile. It was an indescribable feeling.*

One way to capture precious moments is to consciously slow

the frantic whirl of activity that makes up so much of our life. Stop moving, stop talking, stop thinking. Breath slowly and deeply, inhaling the fragrance and texture of an individual moment. Feel the sun on your face, the wind brushing through the hair on your arm, the touch of your child's hand, the smell of your newborn's cheek. It is here, in these particular moments, that we are most profoundly alive and can connect most deeply with our children.

> *It started when my son was very young. His mother worked late Friday nights, so at the crack of dawn on Saturdays when he woke up, I would hurry him into his clothes and take him down to a little coffee shop a few blocks away so she could sleep in. It soon became a tradition we both look forward to—here we are, fifteen years later, and still eating breakfast together every Saturday. The only difference is that now I'm the one who has to wake him up.*

A powerful means of filling our children's lives with precious moments is through family rituals and traditions. Born in the earliest days of our species' emergence into consciousness, rituals are the markers we use to carve out a brief time of significance from the nonstop flow of daily life.

> *Every night I tuck her into bed and give her a kiss on both cheeks and her forehead. I used to say, "Do you know who loves you?" and she'd say, "Daddy!" Then I'd say, "Do you know how much I love you?" and*

she'd say, "No." And I'd say, "More than you can
imagine." Now when I ask her if she knows how much
I love her, she says, "More than I can imagine."

Sometimes, like the grace we say before a meal, such rituals
are meant to remind us that the small things we take for
granted are actually daily miracles to be thankful for. Other
times, like the private rituals and code words we use, they are
to remind us of the deep connection that lies just beneath
the surface.

I call my daughter every night when I'm not home
with her. We got into this tradition of saying good
night and good-bye. Originally, it went like this:
    "Goodnight, and don't let the bedbugs bite."
    "I'll tell them, 'No, No, No, you can't bite me or
Daddy.'"
    "Sleep tight."
    "I love you."
    "I love you, too."
    "Good-bye."
    "Good-bye."
Then it was abbreviated to:
    "Good night, and don't let the bedbugs bite."
    "Good night, and all the other stuff, Daddy."
    "Good-bye."
    "Good-bye."
Now it has become:
    "Good night and everything."

"Good night and everything."
"Good-bye."
"Good-bye."

Sometimes, such personal rituals, like celebrating birthdays, bar mitzvahs, and special events, are meant to honor momentous rites of passage. At their core, the purpose is always to publicly mark and hold onto a single moment: by bringing us together, by reweaving the powerful threads of connection, by reminding us that as much as we are all very much alone, so too we are all bound up in this life together.

When my son was five, we had a typical kid-birthday party, and something about it really bothered me. All the kids had a good time, but it was complete kid chaos of playing, screaming, and eating. I wanted to do something that felt more personal, so we had a birthday dinner; and after we finished eating, we went around the table, everyone telling a story that had the birthday boy playing the starring role. My kids are great, big teenagers now, and they roll their eyes as birthdays approach and say things like, "Do we have to do that again?" But the truth is they love it, and it has been the occasion of many a beautiful moment.

The ways we choose to observe and honor our connections with our children will evolve as we grow, but we will never stop being their father.

My father died after a very painful fight with cancer. I was at his side, worrying, and he reached over, squeezed my hand, and said, "It's really OK, son." Then he said he was tired and wanted to rest a few minutes, and that was it. He was dying, he was wracked with pain, and he was telling me it was OK.

When I came out of his room, my son—who had been very close to his grandfather—had just arrived after driving three hundred miles from college. I found myself holding him and saying, "It's OK son, it's really OK."

Fathering is forever. The form and content will evolve and transform over time, but the heart of being a father, the deep emotional bond between a father and his child, continues to exert its power well beyond our lifetime.

My father told me a story that his grandfather had told him about when my great-grandfather had left the old country to come to America. It is a very common story about poverty and dreams and a man who felt he had no other options, but every time that story is told, the simple courage of that uneducated farmer is re-created.

Little did we imagine how broad and deep were the places fatherhood would take us. In the moment we decided to become a father, invisible threads of connection expanded outward, binding us and welcoming us into a vast community that stretches beyond time and comprehension. Part of our job as fathers is to become the human bridge across that expanse for our children. To link them with their past, pave the way to their future, and, in the process, hold and cherish every moment we can.

I have two children from my first wife, two stepchildren that I have raised as my own since they were very young, and now we have an adopted son. I started a crash course on how to be a father when I was eighteen and here I am, thirty years later. It looks like I will be a full-time father until I drop.

Fathering is different from mothering. We come to our task from the outside, and captured in that configuration is the miracle we have to offer; for true fathering is not the physical act of planting a seed, it is the conscious decision to tend and nourish the seedling. Real fathering is not biological—it is the conscious choice to build an unconditional and unbreakable emotional connection to another human being.

Once that choice is made, it cannot be unmade. We can't abandon our children no matter what the circumstances. We can't simply turn them over to someone else for safekeeping, not even if an ex-wife is doing everything in her power to make a continued connection impossible. We can't wander off for a couple of years to get our lives together or in search of adventure. We can't turn our backs on them if they get into trouble.

The miracle of fathering, the extraordinary power it

possesses to comfort, to heal and to transform, is the manifest proof that as a people, we are not as alone, not as self-
centered, not as alienated as we sometimes fear. It proves
that we can be responsible for one another, that we can
eagerly embrace the often difficult task of fathering this tiny
unknown mystery and finally, that we can and will dedicate
ourselves to caring for one another.

Suggestions for Further Reading

The following books were moving to me in my journey to be a good father and I recommend them wholeheartedly.

Two books by Bruno Bettelheim, *When Love is Not Enough* and *The Uses of Enchantment: The Meaning and Importance of Fairy Tales*, perform the invaluable task of clearly and powerfully articulating the real world as seen and experienced by children. Bettelheim's penetrating analysis provides a unique opportunity to view childhood—our own and our children's—through a window of understanding framed by one of this century's best minds.

How we came to be the way we are, why men and women act, think, and feel the way they do, is a crucial piece of information for any man wanting to be the best father he can be. Unfortunately most of what our contemporary culture offers us in the way of insight on this issue is frighteningly confused and cynical or extremely shallow. Two notable exceptions are Dorothy Dinnerstein's *The Mermaid and The Minotaur* and Daphne Rose Kingma's *The Men We Never Knew.*

Dinnerstein ricochets from concept to concept with abandon. Everything she writes seems to bring up another point she really needs to elaborate on until she quickly overwhelms the usual techniques of parenthetical and footnotes and is forced to sprinkle "boxes" of asides throughout the book. Yet the depth and clarity of her thoughts overwhelm any irritation you might experience at the wild ride. At the root of her thesis is a very simple and revolutionary proposition—that most of the problems in the world can be traced to the fact that women—and women alone—are responsible for the earliest years of childrearing; she makes a passionate case for the need for both men and women to fully participate in childrearing.

Much of what we need to be as fathers cannot be properly understood until we have grappled with the more fundamental issues of what it is to be a man and how we can be deeply connected to a woman. With a gentle compassion that can take your breath away, Kingma patiently and convincingly constructs a bridge over the abyss, showing us the path that can bring us back together. Indeed, Kingma not only builds the bridge, but crosses it to become a fervent and feeling advocate for men.

Closer to home is *Father Love* by Richard Louv which is part manifesto, part confession, and part passionate plea for change. Of all the books out there on fathering, Louv's speaks with the most heart and the clearest vision.

On the more practical level, four books stand out: *The Angry Book* by Theodore Isaac Rubin; *I Swore I'd Never Do That,* by Elizabeth Fishel; *Wonderful Ways To Love a Child* by Judy Ford; and *No Enemies Within* by Dawna Markova. *The Angry Book* guides us through the mind-numbing, sense-blurring sensation of anger into acceptance and forgiveness so that we can move forward with clarity, compassion, and honesty. *I Swore I'd Never Do That* offers the "long view" and reminds us how much of who we are has been taken from our parents and how much of who our children will be will be drawn from our behavior. *Wonderful Ways To Love a Child* by Judy Ford is exactly what it sounds like—a beautifully concentrated set of essays on the ways in which we can deliver our love to our children in a manner they will receive it.

Finally, *No Enemies Within* is a friend to turn to when we need to find a way through a place that seems to be impassable. Markova offers us all the tools we need to shed the armor that hinders our efforts, make the connections that long to be made, and find the courage to be the fathers we need to be.

About the Author

Will Glennon is the co-creator and editor of the bestselling *Random Acts of Kindness* series. A native Californian, he founded and ran the Santa Barbara *News & Review* in 1971 and later went on to law school and a position at the California Trial Lawyers Association in Sacramento. A divorced father of two, Will Glennon has worked hard throughout his life to maintain a strong bond with his children despite the demands of work, joint-custody and travel. He has appeared on numerous television and radio programs as a national spokesperson for *Random Acts of Kindness*. Mr. Glennon currently lives in Berkeley, California. *Fathering* is his third book.

Conari Press, established in 1987, publishes books on topics ranging from spirituality and women's history to sexuality and personal growth. Our main goal is to publish quality books that will make a difference in people's lives—both how we feel about ourselves and how we relate to one another. Our readers are or most important resource, and we value your input, suggestions, and ideas. We'd love to hear from you—after all, we are publishing books for you!

For a complete catalog or to get on our mailing list, please contact us at:

CONARI PRESS

2550 Ninth Street, Suite 101, Berkeley, CA 94710-2551
800-685-9595 • fax: 510-649-7190 • e-mail: conaripub@aol.com